THE ROYAL COMMISSION ON CRIMINAL JUSTICE

The Conduct and Supervision of Criminal Investigations

by **Michael Maguire,**
and **Clive Norris**

LONDON: HMSO

© Crown copyright 1992
Applications for reproduction should be made to HMSO.
Second impression 1994

ISBN 0 11 341054 9

Any views expressed in this report are those of the author(s) and do not necessarily reflect the views of the Royal Commission

Contents

ACKNOWLEDGEMENTS

1. INTRODUCTION 1

2. RESEARCH STRATEGIES 5

3. CRIMINAL INVESTIGATION: DEFINITIONS AND INTRODUCTORY COMMENTS
   Reactive and proactive investigations 7
   The role of uniform officers 9

4. THE CID: FUNDAMENTAL PROBLEMS
   Recurrent scandals: the problem of detective malpractice 13
   The detective 'culture' 20
   The problem of supervision 23
   A separate identity: the 'firm within a firm' 26
   The search for solutions: recent trends and new initiatives 27

5. 'ROUTINE' CID WORK ON DIVISION
   The work environment and pressure for results 32
   Frontline supervision: perceptions of its nature and purpose 35
   Supervision and the prevention of malpractice 38
   Potential 'weak spots' in criminal evidence 44
   Concluding remarks 52

6. HOLMES BASED MAJOR INQUIRIES
   Introduction 55
   The HOLMES system 56
   Weak spots and safeguards 61

7. OFFENDER CENTRED POLICING: REGIONAL CRIME SQUADS AND FORCE DRUG SQUADS
   Target operations: introductory remarks 71
   Organisational features 73
   Investigative strategies 75

	Supervisory structures	83
	Potential 'weak spots' and mechanisms of control	86
	Management information	95
8.	SUMMARY AND CONCLUSIONS	
	Summary of arguments and research findings	98
	Possible ways forward	107
	Concluding remarks: crime control and due process	118
BIBLIOGRAPHY		121

Acknowledgements

As we are not naming the police force areas in which we conducted research, we are unable to thank by name the many officers from these forces who took part in the study and gave us assistance and cooperation well beyond our expectations. As far as possible, we have thanked them informally in person.

Other people who helped us enormously as general informants, sounding boards against which to test our ideas, or patient readers of drafts, include our expert consultant, Colin Evans, senior officers from HMCIC's Office and PRSU, police officers attending courses at our Universities, and academics and others with a good knowledge of policing. It is difficult to name them all and we hope we will be forgiven for any glaring omissions. However, we would like to mention particularly (omitting any ranks or titles!) Graham Anthony, David Aherne, Ian Arundale, Keith Carter, Karen Cherrett, Colin Dunnighan, Keith Emerson, Nigel Fielding, Barrie Irving, Brian Jenkins, Ian Johnston, Jocelyn Kynch, Michael Levi, Lesley Noaks, Gordon Shumack and Pat Tucker. We thank them all – and those not mentioned – for their frank and valuable comments, in this case stressing very firmly the usual rider that any mistakes are ours, not theirs.

Finally, we thank Julie Vennard and Carol Hedderman, of the Royal Commission's Secretariat, for their invaluable support and advice throughout the project.

1. INTRODUCTION

The research project upon which this report is based was designed to assist the Royal Commission on Criminal Justice with its deliberations under paragraph (i) of its terms of reference, namely:

> 'the conduct of police investigations and their supervision by senior police officers, and in particular the degree of control that is exercised by those officers over the conduct of the investigation and the gathering and preparation of evidence'

The bulk of the evidence received by the Commission under this heading refers to issues directly related to the interviewing of suspects in police custody, in particular the adequacy or otherwise of the safeguards introduced by the Police and Criminal Evidence Act 1984. This is not at all surprising, given the circumstances of the particular cases which led to the setting up of the Commission and, further, the centrality of confession evidence to a large proportion of criminal convictions (see, for example, McConville *et al* 1991; Moston *et al* 1990, 1992). However, whilst recognizing the importance of the regulation of detention and questioning, we have not devoted close attention to this specific topic. This is partly because others have already covered the ground thoroughly,[1] but mainly because our focus is a much broader one.

One of the points we are anxious to underline is that interviews are only one among many sources of evidence – eg witness statements, observations by police officers, forensic or physical evidence – all of which are potentially open to error or abuse by a careless, overzealous or dishonest officer. Moreover, interviews do not occur in a vacuum: they often follow 'conversations' prior to, or even after, arrival at a police station, which may have some influence upon what is said later on tape (Moston and Stephenson 1992). Such situations can result in claims that the subsequent admissions were improperly obtained. With the advent of tape-recording, there is less room for dispute about what was or was not said in the interview itself, and it is likely that most future courtroom battles over the validity of evidence will be fought on different ground. Indeed, according to many police officers, lawyers and convicted offenders

---

[1] For studies of the impact of PACE upon the regulation of detention and interviews, see Maguire (1988), Irving and McKenzie (1989), Brown (1989, 1991), Bottomley *et al* (1991, 1991a), McConville *et al* (1991) and Moston *et al* (1990).

we spoke to, the main area of contention has already shifted away from the conduct and content of the formal interview to events preceding it, with increases in allegations of the use of threats or inducements, as well as in challenges to the integrity or authenticity of other types of evidence. As one lawyer put it, 'You squeeze a balloon in one place, it pops up in another'.

A further point we shall emphasise throughout is that not all investigators work in a similar way. There are fundamental differences between proactive and reactive investigations, and between investigations in different areas of crime. For example, the methods used daily by specialist crime squads are unlike those normally employed in divisional CID offices, and the evidence necessary to convict a drug dealer is often of a different kind – and obtained by a different process – than that used to convict a murderer. The groups of detectives undertaking these tasks are also structured, managed and supervised in variety of ways. These differences mean that, while the development of mechanisms for regulating and controlling criminal investigations can be based upon a set of general principles, serious thought has to be given to their applicability in a variety of contexts.

The specific aims set out in our research proposal were as follows:

i. to construct a picture of the types and styles of investigation at different levels in the police organisation, with particular emphasis upon very serious crime,

ii. to ascertain the nature and degree of the supervision exercised in different branches of the police and in different phases of investigations, and

iii. to identify practical problems in the management and supervision of investigations, to look at current strategies for overcoming these and to canvass ideas on 'best practice'.

In order to undertake such a wide-ranging study within a short period of time, we had to limit severely the amount of fieldwork and data collection in each police unit we examined, aiming not for detailed accounts of procedures or rigorous sampling of cases, but for a broad picture of how each approached its investigative tasks, of the relevant management and supervisory arrangements, and of those aspects of its work which appeared to contain the greatest potential for 'things to go wrong'. In the latter case, we were concerned particularly with the possibility – whether by accident or design – of evidence being produced which was either false or improperly obtained and, by implication, of people being wrongfully convicted.

We looked at these matters with a deliberately jaundiced eye, adopting a policy of considering the 'worst possible scenario'. Quite often, we challenged senior officers with questions such as 'How do you know your detectives are not regularly fabricating evidence?' and 'How can you convince me they are not?' or operational detectives with questions like 'What is to stop you threatening people in the car so they confess when you get to the station?' Our report, too, often reflects this deliberate focus on the negative, the possibility of serious errors or malpractice. This should not be taken to imply that we believe such events or behaviour to be commonplace, or most CID officers to be incompetent or 'bent'. As it happens, we do not. But, in a sense, the actual extent of malpractice, even if it is minuscule, is irrelevant to the subject we are tackling: what is important is the *potential* for it to occur, should any officer or group of officers fail to do their job properly, and the soundness of any system designed to prevent it.

The report is structured as follows. In Chapter Two, we outline our research strategies and sources of information. In Chapter Three we introduce the main types of investigative strategy and make a few comments about the significant role played by uniform constables: while our study concentrated exclusively on the work of CID officers, it is important to remember that the majority of crime arrests are made by their uniformed colleagues.

In Chapter Four we draw attention to the history of recurring scandals in the CID and to the formidable obstacles which have to be overcome if the pattern is to be finally broken. We first relate these scandals to some fundamental problems and dilemmas in the task of crime investigation and illustrate a range of competing views about the relationship, and proper balance, between curbs on police actions and the effectiveness of crime control. We then discuss the nature and effects of the 'detective culture', as identified by a number of academic writers, and introduce the basic problem of marrying effective supervision with a style of work in which individual initiative and autonomy have traditionally been regarded as key to the successful detection of crime. We also look briefly at the issue of the separation between the CID and uniform branches. Finally, we mention a range of recent initiatives by the government, Home Office and the police themselves, some of which have tried to address these deep-seated problems: we note that the CID may be entering – or may already have entered – a period of significant change in its history, although as yet the pace and depth of any such change appears to be very variable across the country.

Chapters Five, Six and Seven present the results of our fieldwork in divisional CID offices, major incident rooms, and force and regional crime squads, respectively. In each case, we outline the organisational and supervisory structures, the dominant investigative style and the kinds of evidence typically sought. We also discuss any specific kinds of pressure under which the officers tend to be placed. We then try to identify 'weak spots' – ie areas with potentially the greatest vulnerability to error or malpractice – which are of particular relevance to that kind of investigation, assessing the strengths and limitations of the existing supervisory practices (or other regulatory mechanisms) as tools for preventing such injustices occurring.

Finally, in Chapter Eight we summarise our findings and put forward various options for tackling the problems identified. Most of these build upon ideas currently being floated or implemented by various forces and upon 'good practice' we identified in the course of our research. We also put forward our own idea of 'quality control'. This derives from our central conclusion that the prevention of sloppiness or malpractice in investigations is too dependent at present upon the individual qualities of managers and the integrity of operational detectives. What is required, we argue, is the development of a more impersonal and systematic approach, based upon the concept of random and independent monitoring.

2. RESEARCH STRATEGIES

The findings presented in this report are derived from four main bodies of data: interviews with detectives of all ranks, observations of a number of key activities, examinations of case files, and documentary sources. The fieldwork was conducted in three force areas, two of them covering metropolitan areas and the other a large county force. These are not identified in the report, nor are individual incidents, cases or comments distinguished by which of the three they are taken from.

During the course of the study we spent time at a wide range of CID locations, to some of which we returned several times (for example, five consecutive days were spent with one Force Drugs Squad). These included five HOLMES-based incident rooms (four murder cases and one serial sex attack), three Regional Crime Squad Branch Offices, two Drugs Squads, two Serious Crime Squads, a Stolen Vehicles Squad, a Vice Squad, two Intelligence Units, and five divisional CID offices. Three days were spent observing training courses. We also paid one-off visits to two other forces and discussed recent national developments with members of relevant committees of the Association of Chief Police Officers and with senior officers seconded to HM Inspectorate of Constabulary.

We interviewed over 75 officers, ranging in rank from Detective Constable to Deputy Chief Constable. Although we initially used a structured questionnaire, we quickly found such a fixed format unsuitable, owing to the wide diversity of operational settings, variations in the types of cases they dealt with, and the sensitive nature of many of our questions. Instead, we adopted the policy of conducting informal and only loosely structured interviews, guided by a checklist to ensure that we covered a particular range of topics.

In addition, we engaged in numerous conversations with CID officers in work and social settings, where they did not feel they were being 'interviewed' and hence tended to be more relaxed and open in what they said. Some we got to know over several visits, allowing a considerable degree of trust to be built up. Such conversations, although recorded only from memory rather than (as in interviews) through contemporaneous note-taking, gave us an invaluable 'feel' of the CID world.

In all, the researchers spent over one hundred and twenty hours 'shadowing' officers as they performed a variety of tasks. These included mobile surveillance in connection with drug, murder, and robbery investigations; the management of a large-scale murder enquiry; routine activities such as taking statements from victims and witnesses, executing search warrants, setting up identity parades, and the arrest and interview of suspects; and miscellaneous duties, including policing an 'acid house party' and attending a post mortem.

In each of the main areas of CID work we looked at – 'routine' investigations at subdivisional level, HOLMES-based major crime inquiries, and Regional Crime Squads and Drugs Squads – we generated from investigation files small samples of current or recently completed cases. These were used to provide illustrative material about the particular investigative strategies used to build different types of case, about the kinds of evidence produced, and about potential problems and 'weak spots'. Some of these cases were also discussed in some detail with the investigating officers.

Finally, some use was made of unpublished material from Maguire's previous research study (Maguire *et al* 1992), the object of which was to develop measures for assessing investigative performance. That study entailed research in six force areas, analysis of large samples of crime files and lengthy periods of observation of divisional CID work.

To summarise, given the nature of the topics covered, the scale of the project and the narrow time constraints, we were unable to employ methodologies which would have allowed us to produce findings supported by statistically sound analyses of data. Nevertheless, the approach we adopted generated a wealth of information about elements of policing which have not been closely studied before. It also enabled us to gain a fairly systematic overview of the problematic areas and the views of officers about these. We hope we have been able to convey some of these insights in a reasoned fashion in this report, despite the fact that it, too, had to be written in a shorter time than we required to do full justice to the material gathered.

3. CRIMINAL INVESTIGATION: DEFINITIONS AND INTRODUCTORY COMMENTS

Reactive and proactive investigations

At a superficial level, the majority of criminal investigations can be characterised as the application of a set of standard procedures to reports or allegations that a crime has been committed. Most such reports emanate from members of the public (including commercial and other organisations)[1] and most are fairly easily classifiable at the outset as complaints of a specific type of criminal offence. The investigations are 'reactive', or 'offence based', in the sense that police officers are expected to make appropriate inquiries into each individual complaint, completing forms to satisfy their supervisors that they have done so. Police handbooks usually present this process as a logical and systematic 'search for the truth': in the archetypal case, the investigator undertakes inquiries in order to (i) determine whether, in fact, an offence has been committed and (ii) gather sufficient evidence to establish a set of possible suspects, to eliminate those not responsible, and to support criminal charges against any who might be.[2]

This ideal model of the investigative process underlies the choice of the 'clear up rate' as the principal method of evaluating police performance in relation to crime: in short, the police are presented by the public with a given number of crimes to solve, and the clear up rate shows in what proportion of cases they have been successful.[3] There are, however, numerous exceptions to this pattern of events, which not only call into question the appropriateness and validity of the clear up rate as a measure of effectiveness,[4] but have implications for the management,

---

[1] Studies have generally found that between 80 and 95 per cent of recorded crimes are reported by members of the public: see, for example, McCabe and Sutcliffe (1976), Bottomley and Coleman (1981), Shapland and Vagg (1988), Maguire *et al* (1992).
[2] See, for example, Colman (1989).
[3] The clear up rate indicates the proportion of all officially recorded crimes in which one or more named people have been charged, summonsed, cautioned, or otherwise dealt with on the basis of an admission or *prima facie* evidence that they were the perpetrator(s) – the latter includes TICs and prison write offs (see note 6), as well as admissions by children under the age of criminal responsibility.
[4] For discussions of the shortcomings of the clear up rate, see Burrows (1986), Hough (1987), Bennett (1990), Maguire *et al* (1992).

supervision and ethics of investigations. First of all, some offences come to light in ways other than through official crime complaints by members of the public: the police themselves witness (by accident or design) actions which they categorise as criminal offences;[5] people detained or imprisoned for other matters quite frequently admit to offences previously unknown to the police;[6] and many ambiguous situations or actions are translated, after consideration of evidence or through negotiation, into criminal charges quite different to an initial complaint.[7] It should also be noted that a fair proportion of investigations involve so-called 'victimless' or 'consensual' crimes and hence lack an aggrieved party or complainant.

Secondly, the individual offence based model of investigation is paid little more than lip-service in many instances, particularly where some common 'stranger-to-stranger' property offences (such as burglary and theft from vehicles) are concerned. Unless there are immediate indications of the offender's identity, there is frequently little hope of solving such cases by conventional reactive methods[8] and those attending the scene freely admit that they are often doing little more than going through the motions, the only value of the exercise being to reassure victims that 'something is being done'.[9] It can therefore be more productive in terms of detections to 'start from the other end', i.e. by identifying prolific offenders and using a variety of strategies to discover and demonstrate their involvement in various offences, previously recorded or not. These strategies may include engineering frequent checks, stops and searches of such people, in the hope of catching them with evidence of criminal offences;[10] the use of surveillance or informants to obtain intelligence

---

[5] Maguire *et al* (1992) found that about five per cent of recorded crimes came to notice as a result of police patrols or observation. See also Steer (1980), Mawby (1979).

[6] These are generally referred to either as 'TICs' (when the new offences, though not charged, are admitted in court and 'taken into consideration' in sentencing) or as 'prison write offs' (when offences are officially admitted in prison to a visiting police officer, on the understanding – though not the guarantee – that no charges will be brought). Some, of course, become main charges in court.

[7] Maguire *et al* (1992) found that about six per cent of those charged were charged with a main offence different to that for which they had been arrested.

[8] This has been shown many times, most clearly in a large-scale American study (Greenwood *et al* 1977), where, for example, only one per cent of a sample of burglaries in which no offender had been identified within 24 hours were eventually detected. See also Steer (1980), Maguire (1982).

[9] This has, of course, become an important consideration with wider recognition of the emotional impact upon victims of crimes such as burglary, and the growing influence of the 'victims movement' (Maguire 1982, 1985, 1991; Shapland *et al* 1985). Attention to victims has occupied a prominent place in recent police initiatives aimed at providing a better service to the public (eg the ACPO Strategy Document (1990) and the 'Plus Programme' in London).

[10] A process memorably dubbed 'systematic harassment' by Skolnick (1966).

about their activities; and, whenever they are in detention or in custody, obtaining as many admissions from them as possible.[11] As will be discussed in Chapter Seven, the more sophisticated versions of these 'proactive' (or 'offender', or 'target', based) investigative methods are prominent in initiatives against those relatively invisible – and often consensual – crimes such as supplying drugs, where there is little point in relying upon conventional crime reports from the public.

Thirdly – and highly relevant to the problem of preventing miscarriages of justice – it has been argued forcefully, by McConville et al (1991), among others, that the 'search for the truth' is a mis-description of the process which normally takes place, even in straightforward 'reactive' investigations. A much more common sequence of events, they claim, is that police officers convince themselves, usually at an early stage, that a particular person is guilty and then set out to *construct a case* against him or her. This narrows the focus of the investigation and may lead to contrary evidence being ignored. We shall return to this theme at various points in our discussion.

The role of uniform officers

Despite the importance of offender based methods of investigation – and, in particular, the significant contribution of 'TICs' and 'prison write offs' to clear up rates[12] – it remains true that the majority of crime *arrests* derive from the early identification of suspects in relation to specific offences reported by the public. Two points demand emphasis here. First, this identification is much less often the result of 'detective work', than of the naming or physical handing over of a suspect to the police by a member of the public (an extreme example being the apprehension of suspected shoplifters by store detectives).[13] Second, the majority of crime arrests are

---

[11] Some forces have recognised that prison interviews, in particular, are a rich source of detections, and that one CID officer spending his or her time solely upon such interviews can produce almost as many clear ups as the rest of the office put together (see Burrows 1986; Maguire *et al.* 1992). However, many officers regard this as a pointless statistical exercise, merely a way of 'keeping the bosses happy.'

[12] Since the advent of PACE, TICs have declined considerably in number, while prison write-offs have increased. This is partly because offenders (and their solicitors) regard the latter as a safe and advantageous means of 'wiping the slate clean', while the former contain some risk of a longer sentence. It is also because it is less easy under PACE than it was previously, to 'pump' arrested persons for TICs during interviews.

[13] See Steer (1980); Bottomley and Coleman (1981); Shapland *et al* (1985); Maguire *et al* (1992). The latter found that, in most forces studied, around ten per cent of all recorded crimes entailed the immediate identification of the offender by a member of the public. Estimates of the proportion of clearances produced in this way range from 25 to 60 per cent.

made by *uniform officers*, rather than by CID officers.[14] Uniform relief officers are usually the first to arrive at the scene, where they carry out preliminary enquiries. If there is an immediate suspect, the process of investigation and evidence-gathering can entail little more than the taking of statements from witnesses, the collection of any pertinent physical evidence (eg stolen property) and the location, arrest and interviewing of the suspect. Moreover, although arrested persons are frequently handed over to CID officers for interview, in many forces the majority of interviews and charges are handled solely by uniform officers.[15]

While the focus of this study will be upon the more serious cases dealt with by CID officers, it is important to remember that the 'bread-and-butter' activity of custody units consists of a constant throughput of people arrested and dealt with by uniform officers in this way for relatively minor crimes, together with a significant number arrested for non-index offences such as drunk and disorderly, assault on the police and breach of the peace.[16] (The latter are often the result of self-initiated interventions by police patrols, as opposed to reports by the public). A considerable proportion in both categories are persistent petty offenders of very low social status – the kinds of people we, like many other researchers, have frequently heard police officers refer to dismissively as 'rubbish' or 'toe-rags'.[17] The sheer volume of cases passing through the system, combined with this lack of esteem, tends to place their rights and welfare low on the list of police priorities, thus affording particular importance to the basic safeguards provided by PACE (custody officers, interviewing rules, access to legal advice, and so on).

As we did not explore these 'low level' investigations in any depth, we cannot assess directly how serious a risk of miscarriages of justice arises from the way they are handled or supervised, nor how effective the PACE rules have been in reducing this risk: other studies concerned more than ours with the day-to-day operation of the Codes of Practice will be of assistance to the Commission in this respect.[18] We would, however, draw attention to the possibility that, in practice, some aspects of PACE afford less protection to suspects in such cases than in major investigations. For

---

[14] Maguire *et al* (1992) found that, in all but one subdivision studied, over three-quarters of all crime arrests were effected by uniform officers.
[15] The ACPO Crime Committee found that between 47 and 72 per cent of interviews were conducted by uniform officers.
[16] Bottomley *et al* (1991) found that about two-thirds of all those detained had been arrested for indictable offences, the remainder either being arrested for non-indictable offences or answering bail, being transferred, detained for own safety, etc. See also Brown (1989).
[17] See Norris (1989), Holdaway (1983), Smith and Gray (1985).
[18] See, for example, McConville *et al* (1991), Brown (1989, 1991), Maguire (1988), Bottomley *et al* (1991).

example, although the presence of a solicitor at interviews is becoming almost the norm when grave offences are alleged, over three-quarters of those arrested on suspicion of minor offences do not request or receive legal advice.[19]

We have emphasised the above points, both in order to place our findings in proper perspective and to underline our general argument that any recommendations for reform should take into account the considerable variety of investigative contexts in which they will apply. In the remainder of the report, we shall focus attention upon the numerically smaller, but generally more serious, cases dealt with by the detective branch of the police service.

---

[19]See Maguire (1988), Brown (1989), McConville *et al* (1991), Bottomley *et al* (1991).

4. THE CRIMINAL INVESTIGATION DEPARTMENT: FUNDAMENTAL PROBLEMS

In this chapter we make some general introductory comments about long-recognised problems which are either inherent in the task of crime investigation itself or arise from the traditional practices, 'occupational culture' or organisational structure of the CID. These fundamental problems have all raised their head repeatedly throughout the Department's history, and form an essential background to understanding the practical problems, relating to specific investigative settings, which we shall be addressing over the next three chapters.

We begin with a broad discussion of the problem of malpractice, as evidenced in periodic scandals over the past 150 years. We then look more briefly at the salient characteristics of what has been called the detective 'culture' (or 'subculture'), at basic questions about the supervision of CID officers, and at the problem of the separate organisational structure and 'dual chain of command' to which they are subject. Finally, we draw attention to a number of initiatives currently being planned or implemented, whose main or subsidiary aims include attempts to tackle some of these root problems.

Recurrent scandals: the problem of detective malpractice

Effectiveness versus propriety?

The Criminal Investigation Department has never been far from controversy and disquiet about its conduct and methods of operation. Its early development took place in a climate of suspicion, with considerable opposition to the notion of 'secretive' policing in plain clothes – due partly to negative associations with 'spying' and 'Continental' methods of political control – and was not helped by recurrent revelations of malpractice by detectives.[1] Indeed, it was perhaps half a century after the birth of Peel's 'New Police' before the CID began to be generally

---

[1] Even the official formation of the CID in 1877 took place against a backcloth of corruption charges against three of the four Chief Inspectors of its prototype organisation, the Detective Branch of the MPD (The 'Turf Frauds' – see Ascoli 1979: 143–6) and, despite assurances of stringent controls, the Department was by 1880 again under attack for the alleged use of *agents provocateurs* (Prothero 1931: 100).

accepted even as a 'necessary evil'. This grudging acceptance arose largely as a result of the perceived failure of the uniform police – whose central objective was the *prevention* of crime, principally through the strategy of patrolling the streets – to 'catch criminals', particularly those who engaged frequently in criminal activity and developed a degree of organisation to protect themselves from detection and conviction. This applied equally to political activists: a key boost was given to the growth of the CID by the need for a more effective response to the Fenian bomb campaign in the 1880s.[2]

This contradictory attitude towards the CID – belief in the need for more *effective* methods of crime control, but at the same time concern about their *propriety* – has continued to haunt debates about policing and to frustrate attempts to devise workable rules to regulate the Department's powers and activities. Public concern has tended to wax and wane with the periodic scandals to which the CID has been subject throughout its history[3] – the two most recent peaks of disquiet being occasioned by widespread corruption scandals in the Metropolitan Police Department in the 1970s[4] and the current spate of 'miscarriages of justice.' At such times, attention becomes focused on ways of controlling detective behaviour and protecting suspects' rights, with all the major players in the game – judges, politicians, senior police officers, the media – united in emphasising the importance of strict compliance with rules and the pre-eminence of 'due process'. However, in periods lacking major scandals, the 'crime control' priority has tended to reassert itself, little sustained interest being shown in the methods used to achieve it.[5]

---

[2] This led, in particular, to the birth of the Special Branch (see Allason 1983).
[3] Further series of major scandals emerged in the 1920s and in the late 1950s and early 1960s. For accounts of some of these events, see Ascoli (1979), LSPU (1984). The uniform branch, too, became one of the severest critics of the CID, on the grounds of its perceived lack of discipline and control, its self-proclaimed 'elite' status and its lack of cooperation with the rest of the force – feelings well summed up in Ascoli's (*op cit*) comment that:
'By 1922 the CID had become a thoroughly venal private army'.
[4] See, for example, Mark (1978); Cox *et al* (1977); Hobbs (1988).
[5] The most comforting explanation of this pattern is that the scandals are genuine 'aberrations' – the product, for example, of individual greed or dishonesty, or of poor local management – in a predominantly trustworthy and rule-respecting detective force, and hence there is no continuing cause for concern. At the other extreme, perhaps the most cynical explanation is that the scandals are merely the tip of an iceberg of almost *routine* rule-violation, but society as a whole (including those with the power to expose it) has been prepared to avert its eyes so long as this does not reach really 'unacceptable' levels. According to this view, many of the formal rules governing police dealings with suspects are tacitly accepted by most participants in the criminal justice system to be largely cosmetic or symbolic – the justifying belief being that, if they were followed to the letter, very few criminals would be convicted (for elaboration of this viewpoint, see McConville *et al* 1991).

The recurring scandals have revolved around three main types of malpractice: corruption, fabrication of evidence (including perjury) and the mistreatment of suspects to obtain confessions.[6] These are all directly related, we suggest, to fundamental problems inherent in the two main components of the CID function as it developed historically, i.e. the specialised tasks of (i) obtaining information ('intelligence') about the movements and activities of 'known criminals' and (ii) gathering sufficient evidence to convict such people of specific offences. In attempting to fulfil these tasks, detectives come up against two fundamental problems, on which we comment briefly below:

i. the fact that, in order to obtain information about the activities of 'criminal groups', detectives have to *get close to them*; and

ii. the problem that obtaining sufficient evidence to convict them in court can be extremely difficult if strict attention is paid to their rights and civil liberties.

Of course, detectives also investigate offences committed by people who do not fall into this general category. However, they themselves, like many outsiders, have traditionally perceived the main thrust of their day to day work as a continuing 'battle' with fairly bounded groups of persistent offenders – those they refer to colloquially as 'villains'.

i. 'Mixing with criminals'

Although regulations were drawn up in the early 19th century forbidding police officers to 'mix with criminals' or even to enter licensed premises without permission,[7] detectives have traditionally ignored, or have been exempted from, such strictures on the grounds that they would be unable to do their job successfully without frequent informal contact with known criminals. Information has to be 'bought', either with money (as in payments to informants) or with promises of preferential or lenient treatment (as in informal 'deals' with those facing arrest or charge) or, indeed, through feigned friendship with active criminals. The dangers of this approach, of course, are that officers will get *too* close to particular criminals and will either fall prey to temptation to take money themselves (eg bribes to discontinue inquiries, or even direct involvement in lucrative criminal enterprises) or allow themselves to be used to protect some offenders at the expense of others. The dilemma is well illustrated by the case of Lundy, one of the most successful detectives in history in terms of arrests and prosecutions of major criminals, but also the subject of

---

[6] See Prothero (1931), Cox *et al* (1977), Ascoli (1979), Hobbs and Maguire (1989).

[7] See Critchley (1967). The latter regulation is still in force – Police (Discipline) Regulations, 1952: 1,15.

numerous allegations and lengthy corruption inquiries which, although never proved, eventually forced him into early retirement.[8] It is also encapsulated in the reply of a Detective Sergeant of 13 years' CID experience to a question we put about what he regarded as the most important 'detective skill':

> 'Being streetwise. Experience of life. Being able to mix with villains without crossing the dividing line of dishonesty.'

ii. Obtaining evidence

The second fundamental problem, that of obtaining valid evidence against people the police believe (or 'know') to be guilty, but who cover their tracks well and make no admissions, lies behind the other two kinds of scandal mentioned – the fabrication, 'doctoring' or 'planting' of evidence, and the mistreatment of suspects in order to obtain 'confessions'. Temptation to act in these ways has sometimes arisen out of a distorted sense of public duty (for example, some detectives have convinced themselves that they have a 'mission' to 'clear the streets of evil people') and sometimes out of pure frustration at the prospect of 'defeat'. But, as will be discussed later, more important factors may be the considerable organisational and external pressures upon detectives to produce 'results' and the fact that chances of promotion are thought (rightly or wrongly) by junior officers to be greatly enhanced by 'good arrests'. A particularly insidious feature of such malpractice historically has been its tendency to spread within groups of CID officers: those who use illegal methods may begin by justifying them to themselves and each other as a 'necessary evil' to deal with a small number of 'dangerous criminals', then slipping into a spiral of regular criminal conduct in which they become less and less concerned whether those they 'fit up' are in fact guilty.[9]

Competing views of the problem

Most attempts to explain, and proffer solutions to, the problem of detective malpractice take at least some account of the above dilemmas and pressures, as well as of the associated phenomenon of the 'police culture' (discussed separately below). However, there is widespread disagreement about the extent of such malpractice, the strength of the pressures to become involved, the most effective ways of preventing it, and

---

[8] Interestingly, a recent book (Short 1991) argues that his motives and activities have been totally misunderstood and misrepresented, and that his extreme methods and close associations with high level criminals were geared solely towards the goal of 'thieftaking'.

[9] See Cox *et al* (1977). A similar argument has been applied to the activities of the West Midlands Serious Crime Squad by Kaye (1991), although it should be noted that no criminal charges were brought against officers who served there.

whether greater efforts to control it might have a negative impact upon the 'fight against crime'. These questions, of course, are of direct relevance to our task of identifying 'best practice' in the management and supervision of investigations, and we shall later try to throw some light upon them through our research findings. They are, however, large, complex and contentious questions to which we cannot hope to provide definitive answers here. The most we can do is to set out a series of competing conceptual frameworks within which they have been (or might be) addressed and in the context of which our fieldwork-based findings may be considered. We outline briefly below six broad approaches which have been adopted – either expounded in the literature or expressed to us in conversations and interviews during our research. These can be crudely characterised under the following headings:

i. The 'bad apple' view

Those who hold this view[10] deny that there is any real problem beyond that of occasional individual malpractice from a variety of individual motives: with these few exceptions, detectives investigate crime to the best of their ability within the bounds of the law and of internal regulations. The solution, therefore, is simply to improve internal vigilance so that 'deviant' officers can be identified and punished or dismissed.

ii. The 'internal regulation' view

This view differs from the first in acknowledging that there are structural factors, of the kinds outlined above, which place pressures upon *all* CID officers at times to 'bend the rules' (or worse), but contends these are generally successfully kept in check through effective supervisory and disciplinary mechanisms.[11] The solution, again, is seen to lie in internal vigilance, though ideally combined with open acknowledgement of the dangers and the development of sensitive and supportive supervisory systems to reduce the pressures.

iii. The 'crime control' (or 'state necessity') view

A third view asserts that much of what is called 'malpractice' is not the result of occasional individual dishonesty or failures in control mechanisms, but is *a necessary and (within limits) acceptable ingredient of the routine enterprise of crime control.*[12] This conclusion is predicated on

---

[10] This is very much the 'official' police view.
[11] This is, broadly speaking, the philosophy adhered to by the last Royal Commission and the designers of PACE.
[12] This view was quite often expressed to us in an 'off the record' fashion by CID officers. It is also a view held by many ordinary people and, we suspect, by some politicians and by some people working within the criminal justice system.

the view that crime is a 'dirty game' and if society wants it controlled, someone has to get his or her hands dirty in the process: it is virtually impossible to be an effective detective without *regularly* breaching subjects' rights, at least in 'minor' ways; the police have been placed in the impossible position of being expected to 'put criminals behind bars', but at the same time to abide by regulations and rules of evidence which, if followed to the letter, would prevent them from doing so.

According to this view, we are in a 'zero sum game' – the more one protects suspects' rights, the less effective crime control becomes. As crime control is considered to be the clear priority, there can be only one true 'solution' to the problem of deviance from rules: to abolish many of the rules and give the police a freer hand in the fight against crime. However, people who take this view usually accept the need to appease liberal consciences by maintaining the *appearance* of protecting suspects' rights, so a more realistic solution is for the police, as far as possible, to disguise the truth and for the rest of the criminal justice system to 'turn a blind eye' to all but the most extreme violations.

iv. The 'justice' (or 'due process') view

Adherents of this view agree with the 'crime control' analysis that 'rule-bending' is endemic to CID work and acknowledge that we may be dealing with a 'zero sum game', but come to a quite different conclusion.[13] This is that the balance of priorities should be tipped in the opposite direction: we should be prepared to see more 'criminals' escape justice if that is the price which has to be paid to maintain fundamental freedoms. Moreover, although pessimistic about the possibilities of restraining police malpractice (because the police themselves are seen as prime adherents of the 'crime control' view), supporters of this view tend to advocate deterrent policies such as the strengthening of sanctions against police misconduct and the tightening of rules of evidence.

v. The 'reformist' view

Those who take this view challenge the assumptions behind the 'zero sum game' argument: the problem does not have to be seen in such black and white terms.[14] While accepting that to achieve greater control over police conduct without reducing the effectiveness of crime control is a difficult task, the reformist argues that it is not impossible: the incidence of both serious malpractice and 'routine' misconduct by CID officers can be reduced, even if not entirely eliminated, by a variety of strategies which do not excessively 'tie their hands' in the fight against crime. A prime example

---

[13] McConville *et al* (1991) express this view well.
[14] This view underlies several of the initiatives being developed by progressive policy-makers within the police service (see end of this chapter).

cited is that of PACE, where a significant tightening of the regulation of a key investigative tool – the interviewing of suspects – does not appear to have had drastic effects on the numbers of criminal convictions, nor even on the numbers of confessions. At the same time, it has considerably reduced the incidence of mistreatment of suspects in police stations.[15]

The reason this can happen, reformists argue, is that the closure of unethical, and essentially 'lazy', avenues for solving the problems of information and evidence gathering (such as putting heavy pressure on people during interviews to inform or confess) gradually encourages detectives to improve their other skills and to put more effort into alternative avenues, such as more efficient use of technology, more thorough searches for witnesses and better preparation of interviews.

vi. The 'radical reformist' view

Although also optimistic about the possibility of reducing malpractice without losing effectiveness in crime control, the 'radical reformist' is sceptical of the extent to which meaningful changes can be achieved through regulatory mechanisms such as PACE.[16] What is necessary, he or she argues, is a full-scale, long-term revision of traditional ways of thinking about investigation and a heavy attack upon the 'police culture'. Through working towards goals such as visibly fair treatment of all suspects and more sympathetic attention to victims, the police will eventually win the confidence and cooperation of the essentially 'law-abiding', but currently alienated, communities living in high crime areas, releasing a new flood of information and witness statements about criminal activities and hence enhancing clear up rates. This view, unlike all the others, also implies a challenge to the long-standing view of crime-fighting as necessitating an eternal battle between the police and an almost separate 'breed' (the 'villains'): the majority of those who are currently regular objects of police attentions, it is argued, would in the new circumstances be persuaded to join the majority in condemning crime.

The detective 'culture'

Whichever of the above explanatory frameworks they favour, those who believe that changes in CID investigative practice are desirable have to take account of forces resistant to such change. One major obstacle, it is widely agreed, is what has been identified and documented in numerous

---

[15] For evidence of the small effect of PACE on convictions and confessions, see Brown (1989), Moston *et al* (1990). Maguire and Corbett (1991) confirm that relatively few official complaints are made about treatment received in police stations. However, comparable data pre-PACE are not available.

[16] This view is expressed particularly by the 'left realist' school of criminology (see, for example, Kinsey, Lea and Young 1986)

academic studies as a distinctive police 'occupational culture'.[17] Two of the essential features of this culture are said to be 'solidarity' and 'secrecy', manifested in a strong *esprit de corps* and code of mutual protection among junior officers.[18] This not only makes it difficult for outsiders to penetrate, but helps to maintain a set of informal working practices – largely invisible to supervisory officers – based upon constables' own perceptions of how to do 'the job', in the face of what they see as a myriad of unrealistic formal rules and procedures designed to impose the ideas of an 'out of touch' police establishment. This is well expressed in the classification of the police organisation as a 'mock bureaucracy' (Gouldner 1954) or 'symbolic bureaucracy' (Jacobs 1969), where what appears on the surface to be a highly regulated, hierarchical organisation with almost militaristic discipline, in practice allows a great deal of autonomy and discretion at junior levels, relatively little affected by supervisory officers or formal regulations.[19]

Although not questioning the basic truth of these insights, Punch (1983), among others, has pointed out that they are based predominantly upon observational studies of uniform relief officers, which may have led to a mistaken notion of the pervasiveness of a single 'culture': rather, different different units and branches – as well as ranks – of the police may develop their own distinctive attitudes and behaviour patterns.

Markedly fewer empirically-based studies have been conducted, particularly in Britain, of a specific 'detective culture', although there is useful material to be found in Hobbs (1988), Young (1991) and Smith and Gray (1985). The distinguishing characteristics identified in this literature include even greater secrecy and defensiveness towards outsiders (including police outsiders), but, in contrast to the 'solidarity' of the uniform shift, a largely individualistic and 'entrepreneurial' approach, in which loyalties are fragmented and sometimes restricted to just one or two 'partners'. This is reflected, according to such writers, in a general reluctance to share information, jealous guarding of the names of informants, and competition to take personal credit (or 'glory') for high-status arrests or clearances.[20]

---

[17] See, for example, Skolnick (1966), Holdaway (1983), Smith and Gray (1985).
[18] Other features commonly referred to include the attachment of high value to 'action', adherence to racist and sexist views, and a tendency to view people and events in stereotypical, 'black and white' terms.
[19] See also Skolnick (1967), Manning (1967), Brodeur (1981). It should be remembered, too, that traditional understandings of constables' powers of arrest afford them a great deal of discretion, to the extent that they cannot be ordered by a senior officer to arrest or not to arrest in an individual case (Lustgarten 1986).
[20] These tendencies are apparently not new. Wensley (1931) writes of detectives 'inclined to keep information to themselves' and of those 'with a streak of vanity that impels them to adopt a pose at the expense of those who have really done the work'. He concludes, however, that individual enterprise remains as important as ever to the success of the CID.

Another commonly identified feature is detectives' willingness regularly to 'sail close to the wind' where formal rules are concerned – encapsulated, for example, in office jokes about the 'Ways and Means Act'. The alleged greater confidence among detectives than among uniform officers that rules can be safely 'bent' (if not broken) derives partly from the less visible nature of their dealings with suspects, partly from their greater legal knowledge and awareness (some writers have described them as 'legal entrepreneurs', constantly exploring and testing the boundaries of legal and procedural rules)[21] and partly from the different kind of relationship they tend to develop with supervisors: unlike in the uniform branch, where Sergeants and Inspectors have traditionally been quite hard on technical breaches of procedure by PCs, CID frontline supervisors (particularly Detective Sergeants) frequently carry their own caseloads and work in partnership with DCs. This has not only reduced the distance in rank between the two groups, encouraging personal loyalties and friendships, but has kept DSs 'closer to the street' and hence closer to the temptation not to allow regulations to stand in the way of getting results.

A final image traditionally associated with the CID has been that of the 'hard-working, hard-drinking' detective, whose lifestyle is characterised by long and irregular working hours, many of them spent in the male-dominated social world of clubs and pubs. This image has been presented both positively and negatively: on the one hand, the highly motivated 'thieftaker' prepared to devote all his [*sic*] spare time to the pursuit of criminals in their own milieu; on the other, the drinker and socialiser, less interested in effective policing than in enjoying the freedom and status of the detective lifestyle.

A discussion of the 'detective culture' would not be complete without some remarks about the ways in which new and prospective CID officers 'learn the job', in terms of both investigative skills and the values and attitudes which shape the way these skills are applied. The role of detective training is clearly of relevance here, but as others are exploring training issues on behalf of the Royal Commission, we shall do no more than make a few general points on the subject. In doing so, we recognise that the Central Planning Unit, which is responsible for designing model courses for use or adaptation at force or regional level, is currently considering radical changes to the traditional pattern.

First of all, the ten-week junior detective training course, which all new CID officers are expected to attend, has since its inception been dominated by the teaching of criminal law and the rules of evidence,

---

[21] See, for example, Skolnick (1966), Manning (1977), McBarnet (1981), McConville *et al* (1991).

together with some consideration of psychological techniques for persuading suspects to make admissions (cf. Morgan 1990). One DS we interviewed characterised the underlying aims of the course he had attended (admittedly, several years ago) as to equip him with the knowledge to 'use the law as a weapon'. He gave the example of the offence of possessing an offensive weapon, proof of which required more than simply demonstrating possession of, say, a knife: he had been taught to induce anyone found carrying a knife to state that it was for their own protection (which constituted sufficient evidence for the offence), by means of remarks such as 'I suppose this is a dangerous area to walk around in'.

By contrast, at least until very recently, comparatively little attention has been paid on training courses to the ethical and practical problems of investigating crime or, in particular, the dangers of wrongful conviction. Similarly, advanced CID courses have equipped higher ranking officers with detailed knowledge about new techniques, particularly in relation to major crime investigations, but have concentrated far less upon 'nuts and bolts' issues such as how to check the quality and integrity of the work of DCs. Of course, DSs and DIs also attend generic promotion courses, in which supervisory issues are prominent, but these tend to be dominated by discussions of the somewhat different situations faced by uniform sergeants and inspectors, who make up the majority of those taking part.[22]

Moreover, owing to pressure on time and the reluctance of senior officers to release them, many CID officers do not attend courses until some time after they have taken up their posts. This applies both to new detective officers (a high proportion of whom have already been working as aides or fully fledged DCs for some months), and to DSs and DIs, some of whom, we discovered in one force, had not attended promotion courses until more than a year after their elevation. By this time, officers tend to feel that they have already 'learnt the job' by experience. In the case of DCs, this is achieved largely through working with, talking to and observing the practices of more experienced colleagues, a process more describable as 'apprenticeship' or 'socialisation' than as 'training'. The formal course may subsequently appear to be of marginal relevance to the 'reality' they have already experienced, and trainers are faced with a difficult task in convincing them of the undesirability of any dubious habits they may have acquired.[23]

---

[22] See Irving and Dunnighan (1992). At the regional training (promotion) courses we attended, CID officers were in a small minority, and criminal investigation (and its supervision) played a small part in the curriculum.

[23] Among the 26 officers interviewed by Maguire *et al* (1992), over three-quarters rated 'experience' as more important than training in having taught them the basics of the job.

The problem of supervision

In the light of the above overview of long-standing problems associated with the CID, we can now move to a preliminary consideration of one of the central issues of this study: the role of supervision in reducing the chances of errors, 'rule bending' or malpractice in crime investigations and, ultimately, of miscarriages of justice.

Supervision has always been a problematic area in all kinds of policing, mainly because of the high degree of discretion exercised by constables in dealing with situations outside the police station[24] and the 'invisibility' of many of their actions to sergeants and inspectors. It has also been shown that increasing administrative workloads for sergeants have tied them more and more to the station, hence reducing the extent and quality of supervision on the streets.[25] Partly for these reasons, the focus of supervisory attention has largely been concentrated upon the *product* of police work, rather than the activity itself: in a nutshell, the first priority has been to ensure that 'the paperwork is right'. Supervision in this respect can be very thorough and disciplinarian, particularly where young uniform constables are concerned. However, so long as officers are producing 'process', filling in their pocket books adequately and not attracting complaints, relatively little interest has traditionally been shown in how they are actually relating to people or performing their job 'on the streets'. It is only in recent years, stimulated by persistent criticisms of officers' manner in dealing with the public and of insufficient attention to the feelings of victims, that serious efforts have been made to monitor and improve this aspect of their work (see below).

Much less has been written about front-line supervision in the CID, but the indications are that, not only do parallel problems exist, but both the special nature of the work and traditional views about the respective roles of DSs and DCs make effective reform particularly difficult to achieve.

Formally, front-line supervision of Detective Constables is undertaken by Detective Sergeants, who are in turn accountable to Detective Inspectors. The overall ratio of DSs to DCs is considerably higher than that between the equivalent ranks in the uniform branch. We calculate from recent returns to HM Inspectorate of Constabulary that the average CID ratio across all forces except the MPD is 1:3.8, ranging from 1:2.9 to 1:4.7 in individual forces. By contrast, there are about nine PCs for every uniform sergeant. However, within the CID, divisional offices have lower ratios than specialist squads and are often handicapped further

---

[24] See note 19 above.
[25] See Chatterton (1987).

by abstractions and delays in postings: in practice, CID offices typically have one DS for every four to six DCs.

Paradoxically, despite these higher supervisory ratios, it was virtually unanimously asserted by the officers we spoke to that there is 'less supervision' in divisional CID work – and in some CID squads – than in the uniform branch. Several went further, claiming that there is effectively *no* supervision in many areas of detective work. Over the next three chapters, we shall qualify these remarks by looking at specific investigative styles, in some of which supervision is more prominent than in others. We shall also explore in more detail what officers understood by the concept of 'supervision'. At this stage, we are concerned only to emphasise three general points, which together raise a set of challenging questions about its effectiveness.

First, if it is accepted that effective investigation requires detectives to make frequent informal contact with 'criminals' and to follow up any information which may emerge, they must be allowed freedom to move around, sometimes over a wide area, without the handicap of seeking permission for every step. They will therefore, for much of the time, be working on their own or with a partner, often without supervisors having any idea where they are.

Secondly, recognition of this basic fact has helped to entrench a belief among CID officers of all ranks that 'supervision' in the context of detective work is of necessity different to that in the uniform branch: it has to be based on *trust*, rather than upon 'checking up on people.' This view is reflected in the fact that one of the widely agreed criteria for acceptance into the CID in the first place is an officer's 'ability to work with the minimum of supervision'. As a consequence – a point we shall illustrate later – the qualities which are regarded within the CID as marking out a 'good DI' or 'good DS' tend to focus around the concept of *leadership* (such as the ability to motivate, or the courage to take risky decisions), rather than the capacity to ensure strict compliance with rules.

In sociological terms, this style of supervision fits well with Weber's notion of the 'charismatic' mode of authority, which he contrasted with the 'bureaucratic' (or 'rational-legal') mode. It is characterised by an emphasis on flexibility, individual personality, leadership qualities and management by example, as opposed to adherence to formal rules, conformity and standardisation of practice. The former mode is also associated with another feature of CID work we have already identified – a tendency for *apprenticeship*, rather than training, to constitute the main form of induction into the skills of the job (the 'college of the streets' or 'what you can't learn in training school').

The third point is that, in line with this charismatic mode of authority, DSs (and, to a certain extent, DIs) rather than moving into a totally distinct supervisory or managerial role, have traditionally continued to play a prominent part in operational detective work themselves, including carrying their own individual investigative caseloads. This means that for much of their time they are engaged in duties, similar to those of DCs, which eat into the time they might devote to supervision. It can also have a psychological effect on the nature of the supervisory relationship. 'Working' DSs can come to be regarded, or to regard themselves, almost as 'one of the boys': they are engaged in similar activities to those they supervise, often working as a 'partner' with a DC, which tends to reduce the distance between the ranks, create personal loyalties and involve them emotionally in cases. All these factors work in the direction of pushing the supervisory role into second place behind the job of clearing up crime.

Assuming the general truth of the three main points made above (we shall try to assess their applicability to particular situations in the following chapters), the obvious question they raise is the following: what happens if DCs either perform investigations in a sloppy manner or, worse, begin to abuse their trust by 'bending' or breaching rules designed to protect the rights of suspects? At the extreme, to what extent is the 'charismatic' mode of supervision capable of detecting and preventing a slide into a spiral of misconduct, moving from occasional rule bending to systematic abuse of procedures and, ultimately, to outright criminal behaviour?

If such practices involve only one or two officers, the slide *may* be checked by firm action on the part of a vigilant supervisor, or by the complaints procedure. However, if they become endemic, the lesson of history appears to be that supervisory safeguards may well prove inadequate to deal with the problem. This is what appears to have happened in many parts of the CID in the Metropolitan Police Force in the 1970s and is alleged to have occurred in the West Midlands Crime Squad in the 1980s.[26] In such cases, radical measures have had to be applied, including the disbanding of squads and disciplinary action on a considerable scale.

Such cases have raised the further uncomfortable problem that misconduct may emanate from, or be condoned by, supervising officers themselves, at the extreme causing a state of 'rottenness' throughout whole detective units. Analyses of the reasons behind known examples suggest that one major contributory factor has been the operational role played by supervisors: they have become subject to the same pressure as DCs to achieve 'results' and appear to have lost all sense of 'distance' and

---

[26] See Cox *et al* (1977), Kaye (1991).

objectivity. If these analyses are correct, the appropriateness and effectiveness of the present managerial and supervisory structures are called into serious question.

To sum up, we have raised in this preliminary discussion one of the central policing-related questions facing the Commission: whether the traditional modes of supervision in the CID are adequate to prevent repetitions of the kinds of scandal which have periodically tarnished its reputation, or whether more formal (or 'bureaucratic') mechanisms of control, less dependent upon the individual, are necessary. In the next three chapters, we shall use our fieldwork experience to explore the reality of supervisory practice in a variety of investigative contexts, seeking to establish (a) whether it is always, in fact, as dependent upon individual qualities as we have assumed in the above discussion and (b) to what extent it appears weak or strong in relation to specific aspects of detective activity.

A separate identity: the 'firm within a firm'

A final problematic issue which has been raised repeatedly over the years is that of the organisational barriers between the CID and the uniform branch and the associated self-image of detectives as members of a separate and 'elite' organisation – a 'firm within a firm'.[27] One of the key manifestations of this problem is the dual chain of command under which most detectives work. Divisional CID officers, as the name suggests, form part of the personnel of a particular police division and hence, although in a separate 'department', are responsible through the local chain of management to the divisional commander, usually a uniform Superintendent. At the same time, however, they have their own separate line of management into force headquarters, to the Head of CID (Chief Superintendent), who in turn reports to the Assistant Chief Constable with responsibility for crime.

This dual chain of command has generated periodic controversy and argument, exacerbated by traditional rivalries between the CID and uniform branches and resentment by the latter of the tendency of CID officers to by-pass local uniform branch structures, thus behaving almost as a separate police force. As we shall see, some forces have recently taken steps to strengthen local management control over the CID at the expense of the links with headquarters – or, at least, to separate out the different areas of responsibility – but the fundamental problem remains unsolved.

---

[27] The history of this phenomenon is well described by Ascoli (1979).

The search for solutions: Recent trends and new initiatives

Having enunciated a set of fundamental problems which have accompanied the development of the CID, underlying many of the events which have periodically sapped public confidence in its integrity, it is important to draw attention to a number of recent initiatives, some involving legislation and some internally generated by the police, which have had as their main or subsidiary goal the finding of solutions to these problems. Not surprisingly, given the blows which police credibility has suffered in recent years, there are clear signs, particularly in senior police circles, of 'a climate for change'. Indeed, many police officers we spoke to argued that the necessary change has already occurred and that the whole discussion, as we have framed it above, is 'out of date': the character of the CID has changed radically, adequate safeguards have been introduced and the chances of history repeating itself are virtually nil.[28] We shall comment in the following chapters on the general impact at 'ground level' of specific initiatives and of broad shifts in thinking among policy-makers. Here we shall limit ourselves to a brief overview of the developments which have been taking place.

Undoubtedly, the single development which has had the greatest effect upon the day-to-day work of the CID in recent years is the implementation of the Police and Criminal Evidence Act 1984 – in particular, the rules outlined in the Codes of Practice relating to detention and questioning. The main purposes of these rules were to clarify the limits of police powers and the rights of suspects, and to regulate the detention and questioning of suspects by a tight record-keeping system under the control of a supervisory officer (the custody officer) not involved in the investigation. There is, of course, widespread disagreement over the effects the Act has had, ranging from those who assert that the rules have merely spurred CID officers to devise new and devious ways of subverting and circumventing them, to those who believe that PACE has prompted a sea change in police practice and provides genuine protection of suspects' rights.[29]

---

[28] Many, too, it should be noted, put forward the 'bad apple' thesis, insisting that past scandals have been isolated and exaggerated in importance: 'the past', they argued, was not as bad as it has been painted, except in a few 'problem areas' like specialist squads in large cities. Most 'ordinary' divisional CID offices, they claimed, have always acted with a high level of integrity, making the reforms referred to (including much of PACE) largely unnecessary.

[29] Among researchers, McConville *et al* (1991) tend to the former view, while Maguire (1988), Brown (1989), Irving and McKenzie (1989) and Bottomley *et al* (1991) – while by no means coming to the opposite conclusion – all found at least some evidence of genuine change.

Within the police, perhaps the most significant ideological development has been (or will be) the promulgation at very senior level of a new 'ethos' for policing, symbolised in the use of the term police 'service', rather than police 'force'. This is expressed succinctly in the ACPO Strategic Policy Document (1990) and the accompanying Statement of Common Purposes and Values. It is based on the idea of 'quality of service', emphasising the need to develop more 'professional' attitudes and behaviour, integrity, openness, attention to the quality of contacts with members of the public, and willingness to respond to 'well-founded criticism'. While high level pronouncements of this kind may remain at the level of rhetoric, their importance lies in the incorporation of their values into new initiatives and policy reviews on particular topics. One of the most comprehensive attempts to operationalise these principles has been the 'Plus' Programme in the Metropolitan Police Department, in which they have been systematically applied in a linked series of policy reviews and subsequent implementation programmes.[30]

Where CID work is concerned, one important trend can be seen in efforts to move away from the traditional heavy reliance upon individual confessions, towards systems of 'crime management', in which emphasis is placed upon the rational use of crime intelligence and patterns of reported crime to assist the gathering of other forms of evidence against active offenders. This entails more attention to setting priorities, forward planning, teamwork and the sharing of information. As we shall see, while many forces are attempting to apply these ideas, there are numerous practical obstacles to their achievement.

A further set of initiatives revolves around the notion of making Detective Sergeants more like supervisors and less like 'better paid DCs'. A leading development in this area is the Crime Investigation Priority Project ('CIPP'), again in the MPD, which has resulted in a reorganisation of divisional detectives into small teams, each led by a DS, as well as a specially designed training programme to reinforce the ideas behind it.[31]

Another progressive trend has been manifested in efforts to bring the CID and uniform branches closer together. This applies not only to the encouragement of closer working partnerships at ground level, but to the strengthening of lines of communication and responsibility between divisional commanders and their local CID managers. Many forces are now reinforcing the principle that, while decisions about the investigation of major crime remain primarily the responsibility of the force's head of

---

[30] See MPD (1991). The programme consists of nine components, including 'rewards and sanctions systems', 'paperwork and bureaucracy', 'visual appearance of the service', 'performance indicators' and 'communication'.
[31] See CIPP (1989), Gibb-Gray (1990).

CID, the setting of local policies, goals and priorities in relation to 'street crime' are very much the province of the divisional commander. There are also noises being made in some forces about the possibility of breaking the mould entirely, by severing traditional lines of command between divisional and headquarters CID officers. Supporters of this move argue that there is no need for a specialist CID management team at headquarters: local DIs should be responsible solely to their divisional commanders, thus being incorporated into a single chain of command and accountability.

There are signs, too, that the emphasis in CID training is shifting from the traditional inculcation of law to broader-based courses which recognise both the practical and the ethical problems facing detectives and set out to equip them with skills to handle them. This topic is covered in another research report to the Royal Commission (Irving and Dunnighan 1992).

Finally, mention should be made of the numerous general 'CID Reviews' which have been undertaken in recent years by individual forces, including those we studied. Many of these have produced ideas and recommendations relevant to the problems we have been discussing, particularly in the areas of supervisory roles, selection and recruitment, tenure, promotion, integration with the uniform branch, and more efficient crime management.

One general point which applies to many of these initiatives is that they have been as much, if not more, driven by concerns about *effectiveness* as by concerns about possible malpractice or wrongful convictions. This stems, to a large extent, from the government's Financial Management Initiative, which has affected the police increasingly since 1983, and has been given momentum by the development of performance indicators by the Office of HM Chief Inspector of Constabulary and by critical attention from the Audit Commission.[32] It can be argued that solutions to the two types of problem complement each other – i.e. that the rationalisation of procedures and the collection of management information necessary to improve 'efficiency and effectiveness' are also useful supervisory and regulatory tools. On the other hand – an issue we shall explore later – it may be that the 'pressure to perform' has a negative effect on the care taken to check evidence or on the scruples of officers.

---

[32] See, for example, Sinclair and Miller (1984), Reiner (1988), Burge (1989), Love (1990), Audit Commission (1990), Maguire *et al* (1992).

5. 'Routine' CID Work on Division

We turn now to practical issues directly related to the management and supervision of investigations undertaken by CID officers. We shall divide our discussion into two main parts. In this chapter and the next, we shall focus upon reactive (offence based) investigation in the context in which it most often takes place, the divisional or subdivisional CID office. In Chapter Seven, we shall look at proactive (or offender based) investigation, as carried out by specialist squads at force or regional level. Reactive investigations will be subdivided into, on the one hand, those undertaken on a 'routine' basis by individual detectives on subdivisions and, on the other, major crime investigations run from incident rooms, some of which are managed or assisted by senior officers from force headquarters, and which may be supplemented by temporary transfers of CID officers from other areas. The latter include investigations using the HOLMES computer system, to which we shall devote particular attention in Chapter Six.

In each of the above contexts, our basic approach will be to give a flavour of the kinds of work being conducted and to identify possible 'problem areas' or 'weak spots' – in organisational structures, in supervision, in the manner in which officers approach their tasks, and in the kinds of evidence they rely upon to obtain convictions – inasmuch as these factors could affect the quality, propriety or procedural correctness of investigations and, ultimately, the justice of their outcomes. We shall also comment briefly on instances of 'good practice' we came across, although wider discussion of optimum strategies will be left until Chapter Eight.

It is worth reiterating at this point that – partly in response to the recent spate of 'unsafe conviction' cases, but also, over the longer term, to the advent of PACE – many forces have engaged in major CID reviews and some significant changes in practice have occurred and are continuing to occur. The fact that change takes place at different speeds in different forces makes it difficult to generalise from findings in three forces. However, as our primary interest is in the *potential* for matters to go wrong, and for particular supervisory or other internal mechanisms to prevent this, it is of secondary importance to our study to know precisely what stage reforms have reached.

The work environment and pressure for 'results'

Officers based in divisional or subdivisional CID offices undertake a certain amount of proactive work, 'targetting' active offenders identified by their own informants or through force intelligence systems. They also sometimes use analysis of crime patterns to focus investigative effort. As noted in Chapter Four, greater use of both these methods of working, which emphasise rationality, forward planning, teamwork (including greater cooperation with uniform officers) and the sharing and structured use of information, is currently being encouraged by ACPO and HMICs and has been recommended in several internal force reviews.[1] However, the pressures and unpredictability of demands upon the time of detectives in all the CID offices we visited, in the course of this and previous research (Maguire *et al* 1992), made it extremely difficult for them to get any but the most modest proactive initiatives off the ground. Work patterns remained essentially those identified consistently in the academic and police literature. Individual officers spent much of their time working on a stream of undetected cases allocated to them by DSs, many of them residential burglaries and miscellaneous thefts. These tended to embroil them in numerous routine (and often unproductive) visits to the scenes. They were also regularly required to interview suspects arrested by uniform officers for relatively minor crimes, which could later tie them up in 'paperwork' (including tape transcriptions) for lengthy periods. At the same time, they were subject to frequent instructions or requests to 'drop everything' and help out with other officers' arrests, ID parades, subsidiary tasks for major inquiries, and so on.[2]

Despite the now widespread implementation of policies – such as the creation of Administrative Support Units and crime screening systems – designed to free detectives from the pressure of paperwork and unproductive use of their time, most of those we spoke to claimed to have noticed little benefit in terms of increased time for proactive work and the cultivation of informants. The general feeling was that such changes had merely slowed a continuing increase in workload generated by rising crime rates and new resource-intensive demands, such as an 'explosion' in child sex abuse cases: as one DS put it, 'We have to run to stand still'. While claims of this kind have to be treated with some caution,[3] there is no doubt

---

[1] For example, Kent, Thames Valley and South Wales.
[2] A similar pattern was found many years ago by Crust (1975). See also Steer (1980), Maguire *et al* 1992. CIPP (1989) found that under five per cent of detectives' time was spent on proactive work.
[3] Anyone interviewed about his or her workload, in whatever profession, will tend to exaggerate its size.

that the typing of tape summaries and transcriptions, in particular,[4] has come to occupy a considerable proportion of CID officers' time, while in every office we visited, overtime credits were running at high levels.[5]

In sum, divisional detectives' work patterns are governed, first and foremost, by a heavy but unpredictable flow of tasks which, although predominantly 'routine' in nature, often require a quick response. This not only allows them little opportunity for planning ahead, but puts pressure on them to expedite the matter in hand quickly and move on to the next task, thus making it difficult, if not impossible, to deal as thoroughly with every case as they might wish. At the same time, it is important to note that by no means all the cases DCs deal with on their own (or with a partner) concern 'run of the mill' offences. In the large city forces we visited, in particular, individuals were quite often allocated serious assaults or large-scale burglaries and 'left to get on with it'.

A further factor which looms large in the working environment of divisional CID offices is that of pressure to produce 'results'. This can take a number of forms. As noted earlier, the main currency by which success is measured in divisional crime work is the 'clear up'. The need to 'keep the Home Office happy', to quote the title of a recent article on the subject[6] (or, one could equally say, to keep police managers happy), by maintaining the clear up rate at an acceptable level, forms a background to the work which can never be ignored.

Although efforts are being made to devise alternative ways of measuring effectiveness and efficiency,[7] the clear up rate remains the key statistic in any assessment of how well a CID office is performing. In interviews with 26 detectives (of DC and DS rank) from six different forces, Maguire *et al* (1992) found that 22 were well aware of the latest rate in their own (sub)division. Moreover, while generally dismissive of its value as an indicator of performance (comments such as 'farcical', 'distorted' and 'open to abuse' being quite common), the majority saw it as a factor which could have a substantial negative impact on the work of the office: any significant fall in the rate was likely to produce not only a

---

[4] This is a new problem since PACE. CID officers often argue that only they can do it properly, as they have the expertise and know the case. They would be reluctant to pass the task to secretaries, even if these were available, or to Administrative Support Units. However, several forces have recently been experimenting with the civilianisation of transcription tasks. Despite officers' fears, this seems preferable to using expensive CID time: the text can always be checked later by the DC concerned.

[5] In one CID office we visited, some officers were over 1,000 hours in credit – they would never actually receive payment for these.

[6] Reiner (1988).

[7] See Audit Commission (1990), Love (1990), Maguire *et al* 1992.

general 'bollocking' from managers and a fall in morale, but efforts to 'massage' the figures back to respectability in a number of fairly artificial (though not necessarily rule-violating) ways.[8] Strategies mentioned – in both that and the current study – included ekeing as many separate charges as possible from minor criminal enterprises, detailing more officers to visit prisons to seek 'write offs', and concentrating more upon 'easy targets' (juvenile and other unsophisticated petty offenders) at the expense of more elusive offenders and more serious cases.[9]

There are also other pressures to 'produce' which become particularly strong from time to time. One occurs when the subdivision is faced with a particular spate of offences which attract media attention: this in turn tends to bring pointed questions from CID managers at headquarters as to what the local DI is 'doing about it'. Other forms of pressure are partly self-generated by individual officers. One mentioned several times was the development of 'workaholic' tendencies, driven by an almost obsessive desire to detect crimes – although older officers claimed that this was now becoming a rarity among the 'new generation' of detectives, who tended to see investigative work 'more like a nine to five job'. A more common driving force, it was said, was ambition for promotion. The desire for promotion may lead officers to seek recognition as a 'good thief taker' (or as someone running a team of good thief takers), which is best achieved either through making noticeably large numbers of arrests or by making some unusually 'good arrests', ie of clever, serious or prolific offenders. As several interviewees remarked, to go before a promotion board with a poor arrest rate is not to improve one's chances – though it should be said that this is nowadays less likely to be a handicap than in the past.[10]

Finally, and probably most important, there is the ever-present threat of being 'put back in uniform' (or, as it was wont to be put, 'made to wear a funny hat').[11] Despite all the rhetoric we heard from senior

---

[8] This applies to uniform officers, too, though to a much lesser degree.

[9] At one CID office we visited in the previous study, we found that, in response to pressure to improve a very poor detection rate, two officers had been employed virtually full-time in activities geared towards 'chasing paper detections' (one on 'prison write offs', one in following up juvenile cases – in which detections had previously been 'lost' as they went to multi-agency panels). Although thus two 'real investigators' short, the office improved its clear up rate significantly.

[10] Senior uniform officers who sit on promotion boards told us that 'managerial potential' was nowadays of far more importance than personal arrest record. This is especially true in forces which no longer allow promotion within the CID (ie promoted officers are automatically transferred to uniform duties).

[11] A final form of pressure – relevant to some squads, but not normally to divisional CID work – is fears for the continued existence of the whole team. This will be discussed separately later.

officers about uniform policing being as valuable as CID work and all being 'part of the same firm', we were left in no doubt that most detectives continue to regard working in the CID as a much more desirable job ('a form of promotion') and transfer back to uniform duties – except on promotion – as an indication of failure. According to several supervisors, as well as DCs, we spoke to, it is this fear above all which 'keeps them working'. At the same time, they recognised, there is a possibility that it will occasionally push some officers towards overzealousness or rule-bending in order to keep their individual results up. The point was nicely illustrated by an ex-DS who recalled a note pinned up in a CID office a few years ago:

'A sus a day keeps the helmet away.'

It also lay behind the interesting reply given by a long-serving DI to a question about what warning signs existed to alert supervisors that malpractice may be occurring:

'I am always most suspicious of the so-called good thieftaker'.

In sum, the working life of detectives in most general CID offices can be characterised, on the one hand, as dominated by the need to keep up with routine tasks – summarising tapes, preparing preliminary case files, visiting the aggrieved parties of allocated crimes – and, on the other, by unpredictability: at any time they can be asked or instructed to help out with colleagues' cases, or 'abstracted' to work on a major inquiry. In the meantime, they are expected – particularly if they have ambitions towards promotion, but also if they are to keep their coveted place in the CID – to 'generate their own work', ie to use initiative to make arrests, cultivate informants and produce intelligence. To some extent, then, they are expected to play a 'team game' (by sharing workloads and information with colleagues, guiding and assisting less experienced uniform officers in the processing of offenders, and contributing to the joint enterprise of maintaining acceptable clear up rates), but there is also a strong individualistic element: they are always conscious that their personal 'resourcefulness' and 'productivity' are being judged by senior officers.

Front line supervision: perceptions of its nature and purpose

We now return to the issue of supervision of the work of Detective Constables. We shall discuss in Chapter Six the somewhat different supervisory arrangements which obtain when divisional officers work as an *ad hoc* team on major inquiries, and in Chapter Seven the supervision of proactive squads, but here we shall concentrate upon the front line supervision of day-to-day CID work on divisions.

We noted in Chapter Four the common assertion among interviewees that, despite the higher supervisory ratios, there is 'less supervision' in the CID than elsewhere in the police service. In exploring the implications of this assertion, it is important to establish precisely what officers understood by 'supervision' in this context. We asked this question many times in the course of observations, conversations and interviews with DCs, DSs and DIs. The answers focussed consistently upon a number of distinct themes, especially:

  i. checking the quality of 'paperwork'
  ii. providing 'leadership' to maintain general morale and productivity
  iii. giving advice and taking decisions on cases
  iv. allocating work equitably and checking that individual officers are not 'skiving'
  v. monitoring overtime and expenses claims

Most of these themes echo points raised in previous studies of the role of uniform supervisors (see, especially, Chatterton 1987): emphasis was placed, on the one hand, upon compliance with administrative rules and the requirements of 'paperwork' and, on the other, upon the encouragement of productivity and diligence; supervision of the quality of contact with the public (including suspects) was hardly mentioned. It was especially noteworthy, given their knowledge that we were conducting research on behalf of the Royal Commission, that few of our interviewees spontaneously related supervision with the ethics of detective work or the prevention of practices which might adversely affect the rights of suspects.

The most frequently mentioned practical means of supervision were the checking of *pocket books* and *case papers*. The frequency and quality of checks on case papers, however, were seen by many to be declining, due to the advent of Administrative (or Operational) Support Units (ASUs/OSUs), which in many forces have taken over from individual DCs the final preparation and collation of files of evidence for submission to the CPS. This has meant that operational DSs tend to leave the monitoring of such 'paperwork' (which, of course, includes statements taken and interviews conducted by the original officer in the case) to the ASU sergeant – who is not necessarily an experienced detective officer.

DSs and DIs claimed to carry out regular checks of pocket books, ranging from once a week to once a month, as well as occasional spot checks. The main purposes were to see that entries were up to date and that individual officers were producing satisfactory levels of activity (out on enquiries, interviewing, making arrests, and so on) and occasionally to confirm the validity of expenses or overtime claims. One DI also said that he checked the sequence of entries containing evidence against the dates of arrests, to confirm that the entries had been made at the right time. It was, however, widely recognised that such checks are unlikely to be an effective means of identifying dubious practices.

In one force, DCs were normally grouped into teams under a single sergeant, but elsewhere supervision of the whole group was the responsibility of whichever sergeant(s) happened to be on duty. The latter system clearly suffered from a lack of continuity, in that it was difficult for each DS to keep track of work allocated by others, but the team system, too, was vulnerable to abstractions and temporary absences of sergeants. Indeed, it is worth emphasising the general problem of both managers and supervisors being absent (at meetings, on courses, on leave, etc). This seemed to be so commonplace in one force that many officers had become used to 'acting' as one rank higher than their own for much of the time. ('We're all members of Equity here', as one put it).

The contrasting degrees of supervision of constables in uniform and CID posts were put down to a number of factors, some relating to the different nature and structure of their work (and that of their supervisors) and others to perceived differences in their abilities. First of all, it was pointed out that a central feature of the work of uniform relief officers is their availability to respond to calls for assistance: they are expected to remain in a limited geographical area and to be in continuing radio contact. They are also often required to return to the station at regular intervals, including to take meals. This means that, at any given time, supervisors can find out fairly quickly where they are and – in broad terms – what they are doing. CID officers, by contrast, are often simply 'out on inquiries', in many cases out of direct radio contact. Although required to give an account later in notebooks or diaries of what they have been doing, such accounts are typically brief and vague.

The other two main reasons given have been mentioned previously: the fact that DSs in most forces, unlike uniform shift supervisors, carry their own investigative caseload and hence find it difficult to keep in touch with what DCs are doing (particularly if the latter are engaged on a complex case, or one allocated to them by another DS); and the general belief that DCs, who have been selected largely on their perceived ability to use their own initiative and work alone, require less supervision. Those making the latter point often argued that uniform sergeants have to supervise relatively high proportions of both 'novices' (probationers and young PCs) and 'time servers' (older PCs who have no ambitions beyond their pension), both of whom require more intensive supervision in order to guard against, on the one hand, errors and incompetence and, on the other, work avoidance strategies; detective sergeants, by contrast, can generally 'trust' DCs both to handle situations competently and to show a higher level of self-motivation. To what extent these latter assertions are sustainable is a moot point, but they undoubtedly form an important plank of the rhetoric surrounding detective supervision.

Supervision and the prevention of malpractice

CID views

When we raised another possible purpose of supervision, that of the prevention of unethical behaviour in the conduct of investigations, the almost standard response of interviewees was to make one or more of the following points:

i. that such conduct, although not unknown in the past, had been largely eradicated by the introduction of PACE and the advent of a 'new breed' of detectives who accepted the restrictions it imposed;
ii. that CID supervision had to be based upon *trust* and *personal knowledge* of officers by their supervisors: it would be both invidious and unproductive to give officers the impression that their integrity was in question; and
iii. that if they were determined to behave in such ways, the nature of the work was such that little could be done to prevent it, at least at the time: as one DS put it, 'You can't go looking over people's shoulders all the time.'

The notion of a 'new breed' of detectives is an interesting one, which we heard repeated in many contexts. The argument was put particularly by senior officers, who claimed that as detectives of the 'old school' gradually retired, to be replaced by younger officers who had 'grown up with PACE', a much more 'professional' CID was being born. Fewer and fewer detectives were now driven by the goal of 'putting away villains' by whatever means possible: the majority were coming to accept that, even when they were certain of an offender's guilt, if sufficient evidence could not be produced they had to avoid any temptation to 'create' it and be prepared to wait for future opportunities to convict him or her in a proper manner. They were also prepared, it was claimed, to put in the harder and more thorough work which such an approach necessitated if reasonable clear up rates were still to be maintained; and they were adapting better to the new styles of crime management which were being encouraged, being more receptive to the ideas of teamwork and shared information.

The other two arguments are interlinked. The last point – that one could not 'look over people's shoulders' – was often qualified by the assertion that, although isolated deviance was difficult to detect, a 'good supervisor' would 'soon get wind of' any *persistent* misconduct. Most divisional CID offices, it was pointed out, are relatively small units in which everyone knows each other and, although DCs tend to work frequently with the same 'partner', there is enough interchange within the group for each officer to get a fair idea of how each of the others operates: any misgivings on this score would soon be transmitted, if only obliquely, to the supervisors. External sources, too, could provide 'feedback' about individual detectives: solicitors, suspects and criminal informants were not slow to let it be known that someone's behaviour was 'out of order'. The following comments of an experienced DS (who often acted as DI when the latter was absent) are fairly typical:

> 'You can never stop deals: that's down to the individual officer. But you can't pull strokes now because people know their rights and their solicitors complain . . . If someone tells me an officer's doing something he shouldn't, I don't necessarily believe it – there's all kinds of accusations flying around in this job and a lot of malicious people out there. But I keep my ears open. If I start hearing the same thing from other people I'll pull him in and put him right in no uncertain terms – we don't want to work with people like that.'

The 'charismatic' style: doubts about its appropriateness

All the above comments and arguments help to confirm our earlier characterisation of the dominant style of supervision in divisional CID work as 'charismatic', as opposed to 'bureaucratic' – ie allowing freedom and flexibility to juniors and dependent for its effectiveness upon the individual personality and qualities of the supervisor, rather than enforcing conformity to rigid formal rules. (More simply, it might be dubbed management 'by example' as opposed to 'by the book'.) The uncomfortable question left hanging, of course, is whether, in the light of past failures, this is 'good enough' – ie good enough both to prevent further serious failures and good enough to reassure a sceptical audience outside the police that this is the case.

Ultimately, it can be argued, the 'charismatic' style of supervision is as good as the people operating it. At its best, a system based upon inspirational leadership, flexibility, trust, close personal relationships and the encouragement of individual initiative has potentially great strengths in terms of producing 'results'. It can also, if the DIs or DSs are sufficiently vigilant and sufficiently firm when necessary, identify and deal with individual officers who are 'sailing close to the wind'. The other side of the coin is its weakness when the quality of the supervisors is deficient (or, being too busy, lose track of what is happening), or when DCs abuse their trust and use their freedom to conceal the fact. In other words, if it can be established that there really is a 'new breed' of detectives who work comfortably within the restrictions of PACE, that all supervisors really do keep a vigilant, if discreet, eye out for any hints of incompetence or malpractice and that, in such circumstances, they take proper remedial action, perhaps the system *is* 'good enough'. If not, it may be necessary to seek more systematic alternatives.

Unfortunately, neither we nor, we suspect, anyone else is in a position to make definitive judgements on most of these questions. It seems fruitless, for example, to become embroiled in a debate about the 'quality' and 'integrity' of CID officers as a whole: senior police officers, as one would expect, tend to say that standards of behaviour and supervision are very high, while critics of the police say the opposite. We are therefore left with only indirect means of assessing the appropriateness and effectiveness of the supervisory style we have identified. The best we can do is (i) attempt to assess the strength of those negative factors in CID officers' working environment which are likely to pose stiff tests of their competence and integrity and thus create a risk that some will fall short of the standards demanded; and (ii) give an impressionistic account of the extent to which the general 'culture' and attitudes of detectives are changing. Although it does not answer the empirical question of how frequently malpractice (or gross negligence, which can have the same result) occurs, this approach has the advantage of directing attention away from the individual qualities of CID officers towards the forces which impinge upon their work. It is only by understanding these forces that one can arrive at an informed judgement on how to best to counteract their influence.

i. 'Negative forces'

The first of the above tasks, identifying 'negative forces' which may test the integrity of officers, has largely been carried out earlier, but it is worth briefly repeating our findings in relation to, first, Detective Constables and, second, supervisory officers.

DCs working 'on division' were operating under considerable pressures to achieve 'results'. These included external pressures on the whole office (to maintain overall clear up rates) and pressures on the individual (to generate arrests in order to ensure keeping his or her post in the CID or, in some cases, to keep alive hopes of promotion). DCs were also operating under pressures caused by the volume of cases they had to deal with and the unpredictable nature of their duties, which made it difficult to direct attention to any one case for as long as they might wish. Under any or all of these sources of pressure, particularly in cases where the officer 'knows' that the person arrested is 'guilty', there is an ever-present temptation to cut corners in investigations, to try to induce confessions by means not allowed under PACE, or to engage in practices referred to by officers as 'gilding the lily' – ie 'touching up the evidence' in various ways to make it stronger (see below).

'Working' DSs – ie those who carry their own caseloads – can come to be regarded, or to regard themselves, almost as 'one of the boys': they are engaged in similar activities to those they supervise, often working as a 'partner' with a DC. This tends to reduce the 'distance' between the ranks, and can create inappropriate loyalties. Although a 'good DS' can handle the confusion of roles and act firmly and objectively as a supervisor when the need arises, there is always a danger – recognised by several of the officers we spoke to – that some will court popularity and shirk their responsibilities.

At the extreme, there is a danger of misconduct being tacitly or openly condoned by supervising officers themselves, including DIs, who are not immune from the pressures we have discussed in relation to DCs: the productivity of the office is primarily their responsibility and any 'successes' or 'failures' in local crime control reflect on them and their careers more than anybody. It should also be noted that many see themselves as carrying a general responsibility to 'keep up the Department's end' within the force as a whole and hence, as one DI put it, may see it as politic to 'consume their own smoke' by dealing with disciplinary issues informally, rather than to put officers on formal reports or to discuss any incipient problems with senior uniform officers in their division.

ii. 'Culture', beliefs and attitudes

The question of whether the CID is a 'changing institution' and, in particular, whether we are seeing the emergence of a 'new breed' of detectives, can only be answered in impressionistic fashion. Our own view is somewhat ambivalent. On the one hand, we remain in little doubt that the 'traditional detective culture' of secretiveness, individualism and belief in the 'Ways and Means Act' is still alive and kicking, particularly in offices containing an above-average proportion of long-serving detectives. We found two or three such officers, who learnt their trade before the advent of PACE, prepared to admit privately to what they saw as 'minor' infractions of the PACE rules (such as taking the 'scenic route' back to the police station in order to speak to arrested people off the record, making 'deals' and offering inducements before tape-recorders were switched on, and employing various psychological tricks) – which they found little difficulty in practising on a fairly frequent basis.

Moreover, it was clear that, although they accepted the major restrictions that PACE had placed upon the 'old way' of obtaining convictions – 'putting them in the cells and sweating them', as one described it – a majority of the CID officers we interviewed, including several senior officers, had not 'internalised' the values of PACE. They followed the rules because they had to, rather than because they believed in them. They deeply disagreed with many of the individual restrictions on their powers and felt that the Act as a whole had unfairly advantaged the more sophisticated persistent offender against the police. A great deal of resentment and frustration was expressed, in particular, about a perceived increase in 'no comment' interviews, wrongly encouraged, as they saw it, by 'obstructive solicitors', who later made matters worse by preparing 'ambush defences' based on stories the accused had by then had time to 'concoct'. There was thus virtually unanimous agreement that the 'right of silence' was wrong in principle: suspects should be obliged to answer questions when interviewed after arrest and if they refuse, this should be taken into account in court. (For detailed discussion of these issues, see Leng 1992).

In other words, if there is a 'new breed' of CID officer, he or she has not been fully converted into a supporter of the 'due process' model of investigation as understood and advocated by most lawyers; the procedures are followed out of respect for the law, not out of conviction that they are right.

On the other hand, two shifts in working practices and attitudes were apparent, which lend some support to the 'new breed' argument. First, there were signs of genuine commitment among junior officers, in principle at least, to the new styles of working, centred around the concept of 'crime management', which are being encouraged by ACPO, HMCIC and Police Divisions within the Home Office. As noted earlier, these place emphasis upon the setting of priorities, forward planning and the rational use of crime intelligence and, if carried out properly, involve regular teamwork and sharing of information – features not often prominent in traditional investigative methods. Crucially, too, they encourage the systematic collection of evidence in advance of arrest – a move away from reliance on confessions. The problem we found, however, was that, owing to practical contraints, the use of such systems currently remains more of an ideal than a reality: developments such as crime screening and ASUs, whose purpose is to free detectives from unproductive caseloads and excessive 'paperwork' so that they can carry out better planned investigations, seem to have made little dent in their routine reactive workloads. Moreover, the continuing importance attached to the clear up rate makes it difficult for DIs to make a wholehearted commitment to such methods, which are geared more towards 'quality arrests' rather than to 'numbers'.

Secondly, it is worth mentioning another kind of change remarked upon by many older officers – one which may sound frivolous, but which actually represents a considerable break with tradition. This is a marked decrease in detectives' overall alcohol consumption and in the amount of time they spend in pubs, both on and off duty.

The trend – which we believe is a real one[12] – may be explained partly by the fact that many forces now take much more seriously than in the past the disciplinary rules against officers drinking on duty and some expressly forbid detectives to enter pubs without permission; and partly by the greater penalties (often, dismissal from the force) now applied to anyone convicted of drink driving. More significantly, it may signal a general shift away from the 'macho' detective culture and, especially, away from traditional ways of 'mixing with criminals' in order to obtain information. (Hobbs 1988, among others, has claimed that most CID visits to pubs and clubs are for enjoyment rather than information, but he also found that detectives maintained informal social contacts with criminals in pubs, which could be developed later.) Indeed, it was frequently said to us that there was now much less informal contact than in the past, to the extent that uniform officers, who are more frequently out of the station, 'know the villains on their patch' better than many CID officers. Some put this down partly to a growing social distance between detectives and the types of 'villain' who form their usual quarry. While the latter still largely inhabit deprived areas of cities, detectives have increasingly become 'office workers' who – thanks to the higher salaries achieved in recent years – live in middle class areas well away from the social world they most often police. Twenty years ago, they were more likely to live closer to it and to spend their evenings in the local pubs and clubs.

To the extent that this is true – and we would suggest that it is a trend rather than a universal change – it is interesting to speculate about the possible long term effects in terms of the problem of malpractice. On the one hand, one might surmise that, with fewer opportunities for detectives to get 'too close' to criminals, the risk of systematic corruption developing has been reduced. On the other hand, it means that information about active criminals has to be sought in alternative ways. One might, therefore, expect a growing tendency to put pressure on those arrested to inform on their peers – raising problems, which will be discussed in the next section, about the grey areas between 'deals',

---

[12] A similar impression was received by the researchers on Maguire's previous study, who spent a considerable amount of time with detectives socially: one commented that more CID officers seemed to spend their spare time jogging and going to gymnasia than in the traditional forum for detectives to 'wind down' (cf. Hobbs 1988).

'threats' and 'inducements', as well as the dubious veracity of information or statements obtained in these circumstances. We shall also return to these issues in Chapter Seven, in the context of styles of policing where the use of criminal informants is of prime importance.

Potential 'weak spots' in criminal evidence

We end this chapter by moving from the general working environment of detectives to their particular task of gathering and presenting evidence. Our aim here is to identify potential 'weak spots' in this process in relation to different kinds of evidence. We shall show later that the kinds of evidence around which cases are built vary considerably according to the type of offence being dealt with and, especially, among specialist branches of the CID: for this reason, the potential weak spots in cases prepared by force Drugs Squads, for example, are generally very different to those in burglary cases dealt with by divisional CID officers. Here, however, our main focus is still upon 'routine' investigations at a local level.

By 'weak spots' we mean those areas in which doubts are most likely to arise, either about the reliability of the evidence put forward or about the ways in which it was obtained. Possible weak spots can be identified by looking at the patterns of defence challenges to evidence in court or simply by asking participants in the system – police, suspects, solicitors, prosecutors, counsel – what they consider to be the types of evidence which give most rise to concern, unease or dispute. It is also important to look at types of evidence which typically 'carry the whole case' – ie, without which it would almost certainly be dismissed.

Criminal evidence can be divided broadly into three main types: admissions or self-incriminating statements made (or alleged to have been made) by defendants; eye-witness or other witness statements; and physical evidence, including stolen goods found in the defendant's possession, documentary evidence (such as bank transactions), fingerprints, and items subjected to forensic analysis. Where 'routine' CID work is concerned, it is well established that the first of these, 'confession' evidence, forms the central plank of a high proportion of cases. While other kinds of evidence are frequently used to support it, there is little doubt that without it the number of successful cases brought would fall dramatically.[13] It is hardly necessary to demonstrate here that this is a potential 'weak spot' in many kinds of investigation – questions about the validity of confessions were of major concern to the 1979 Royal Commission on Criminal Procedure, efforts to regulate and control interviewing practice were central to PACE, and many of the written

---

[13] For example, Moston *et al* (1990) found that about 42 per cent of interviews result in admissions.

submissions to the current Commission focus upon issues surrounding the eliciting and admissability of confession evidence.

However, partly because of the wealth of other material available, and largely because of time constraints on our study, we did not focus much of our attention directly upon the mechanisms designed to control interviewing practice in police stations – the familiar areas of time limits, access to solicitors, the role of custody officers, the use of tape-recording, and so on (see, for example, Maguire 1985; Irving and McKenzie 1989; Bottomley *et al* 1991, 1991a; McConville *et al* 1991; Brown 1991).[14] Rather, we looked at possible weak spots in the regulation and supervision of contacts between detectives and suspects which occur outside the formal setting of the interview room, but which may influence statements or admissions eventually made in that context. These are, principally, non-taped conversations or 'interviews' in police vehicles or other private settings, where possible dangers include the use of threats or inducements to encourage later admissions on tape, and the fabrication or misrecording of statements by the suspect. We also discuss below potential weak spots in two other types of evidence frequently used in 'routine' CID cases: witness statements and police eye witness accounts.

'Deals', 'threats' or 'inducements'? Contact with suspects outside the station

One of the general aims behind PACE – clearly confirmed in the revised Codes of Practice (1991) – was to promote, as far as possible, the use of formal, rather than informal, settings and frameworks for communication between investigating officers and suspects, particularly in relation to statements by the latter which might later be used in evidence against them. Thus, arrested persons must not in normal circumstances be interviewed except at a police station (Code C 11.1), where they should be taken as soon as practicable, and officers must not try to obtain answers to questions by indicating what will happen if they are answered (11.3).

The main aims behind the formulation of these rules were twofold: first, to solve the long-standing problem of 'verbals' – the use, as evidence, of notes of alleged comments made to officers at the scene of arrest or on the way to the police station – arguments about the truth and accuracy of

---

[14] The only point we would make here in passing is one we have not seen made elsewhere: although full tapes are always available to the defence, the proportion of cases in which a summary is accepted is extremely high – indeed, some officers said that they had *never* been asked for a full transcript. This may suggest that the use of unfair 'tricks' and psychological pressure in interviews is now very rare. On the other hand, it may call into question the effectiveness of tape recording as a monitoring device for the conduct of interviews.

which (and about the circumstances in which they were recorded) used to dominate numerous Crown Court trials; and second, to limit the possibility of informal 'deals', threats or inducements being made in order to influence statements made later under formal conditions.

The divisional CID officers we spoke to gave differing accounts of both the extent of informal questioning and the use made of non-taped conversations (for further evidence on these topics, see Moston and Stephenson 1992). Some asserted that they rarely spoke to a 'prisoner' between arrest and formal interview, and would not normally seek to use notes of any conversations as evidence. This approach was explained variously as due to reluctance of the courts to give credence to such evidence; to a local DI's policy that it should not be used; and to the feeling that such conversations only gave ammunition to solicitors to suggest that something improper had taken place. Others, however, thought that this approach betrayed a 'misinterpretation of PACE' and that there was nothing to stop officers informally questioning suspects in all kinds of settings, and recording what was said (for example, they could claim that they were 'obtaining information and [their] explanation of the facts' – Note 11A). And even if the suspect declined to sign the notes and to confirm the conversation on tape, they would still include a record in the file of evidence. In the words of one DC:

'It's up to the CPS and the courts whether they accept it.'

More prosaically, another said:

'You can't just sit in the car in silence'.

It was also asserted by one officer that a detective 'would not be doing his job' if he did not take every opportunity to talk to 'prisoners', although the obtaining of usable evidence was often a secondary consideration: the main purpose was to glean information about local criminal activity and, on occasion, to recruit a future informant (for further comment on the recruiting of informants, see Chapter Seven).

One of the frankest conversations we had on the general topic of car conversations was with a DC of many years' service, who admitted that he regularly took a 'scenic route' back to the police station in order to question arrested persons, although he was well aware that this constituted a breach of PACE and would always deny it if challenged. He would only do this, too, on his own or with individual colleagues he could 'trust'. He recognised that evidence obtained in this way was of little value unless both presented as spontaneous statements by the suspect and corroborated from other sources, but said that it could occasionally 'tip the balance' in a generally weak case. He insisted, however, that he never actually invented or distorted statements made by suspects in these circumstances, although he conceded that there would be little to prevent him doing so 'if I was dishonest'. Several others were prepared to say, in relation to embellishing suspects' remarks, that 'it does happen' (though, usually, 'not in this office'), but the general view was that it was very much less common than in pre-PACE days, not only because such practices now carried greater risks of exposure (because interviews had to be conducted soon afterwards on tape and in the presence of solicitors), but because the 'evidence' thus obtained now carried much less weight in court.

On the question of persuading or putting pressure on suspects to make later statements on tape, officers were careful to distinguish between 'deals' on the one hand and 'threats' or 'inducements' on the other. 'Deals' were generally seen as an inevitable component of detective work: indeed, Hobbs (1988) has argued that its very essence lies in the entrepreneurial 'trading' of favours or rewards in return for information, statements or confessions. Where arrested persons are concerned, the 'favours' might include granting bail, lowering charges, dropping subsidiary charges, or not charging relatives (eg spouses) in return for admissions or information. (Where informants not under arrest are concerned, the reward is often money, but might also include the possibility of ignoring minor offences of which they are suspected.) However, the distinction that many of our interviewees were anxious to stress was that 'deals', unlike 'inducements', were both *voluntary* and *initiated by suspects* rather than by police officers – and hence were not in breach of PACE. For example:

'They always want to deal. When they're arrested they're immediately in the game of damage limitation'.

It was emphasised, moreover, that it was not in officers' power to give firm guarantees that any such favours would actually be granted. All that could be done was to promise to look at the possibilities favourably. (It was pointed out several times, incidentally, that some offenders try to 'deal' for bail, when in fact they are almost certain to receive it – and, unsurprisingly, that officers do not always disabuse them of their ignorance.) It was also recognised that even vague promises of these kinds could be seen as 'inducements' if they were later brought up by the defence, so it was wise either to keep them as 'invisible' as possible, or, conversely, to negotiate only in the presence of a suspect's solicitor.

Where more blatant – ie police-initiated – inducements and, indeed, threats, were concerned, officers were distinctly more circumspect in the responses they gave. It was admitted by several that, 'in the past', it had been fairly common practice in some stations to threaten prisoners that, if they did not confess, they would not be allowed bail, that their wives would be arrested, or even that they would be 'fitted up' for offences (although the threat or use of physical violence was said to have been unusual). The general claim was that the PACE regulations, and especially the early availability to suspects of solicitors, had greatly reduced the opportunities for, and incidence of, crude threats of these kinds and that there was more danger of 'losing' cases – as well as of disciplinary consequences – if they were tried: detained persons were quick to tell their lawyers, as well as to make complaints. Even so, many officers admitted that there were still ample opportunities to engage in such practices if one was determined to do so: the difference was that 'the atmosphere has changed' and they were now seen by supervisors and colleagues, as well as by prisoners, as 'deviant' activities rather than as common practice.

Of course, our information on these matters is based largely upon conversations with police officers, and although we established apparently frank relationships with many – and could draw upon similar conversations with officers whom one of us got to know very well during a previous study (Maguire *et al* 1992) – we are aware that they may still have been concealing a great deal. Several other academic studies, based upon either observation or interviews with police officers,[15] as well as books by journalists, ex-police officers and ex-criminals, have thrown some light on the areas in question, but not only are many based upon events some time in the past, but none can convincingly claim to have accurately assessed the true extent of 'dealing', 'threats' and 'inducements' and it is fair to say that it remains (and may always remain) largely an unknown. Further research, incorporating, for example, systematic interviews with arrested persons and solicitors, might produce new insights, although here, too, there would be serious problems with the reliability of the data. The fact is that we are dealing with a largely 'invisible' area of police activity – itself a major problem for supervisors who wish to monitor what is going on.

Dealings with witnesses and statement taking

A second problematic area, to which surprisingly little attention has been paid, is that of CID officers' dealings with witnesses and, especially, their dealings with witnesses who themselves have some involvement in crime and may not be best known for their truthfulness or for their desire to help the police. Interviews with witnesses are not covered by PACE, although they may take place in police stations if the person agrees to go there. If the 'witness' is suspected of other (or related) offences, hints of the possibility of future police action may persuade him or her to give 'helpful' evidence in the hope of escaping charges. In these circumstances, there is a risk that such evidence will be false, either because the person believes it politic to give the police what they appear to want, or even at the specific suggestion of the police. In other words, the possibility of 'deals',

---

[15] See, for example, Hobbs (1988).

'inducements' and 'threats' arises in relation to witnesses as well as to suspects, though with the difference that the restrictions imposed by PACE do not apply.

It should also be noted that 'helpful', but unreliable, witness statements can be offered to the police, without any inducement, by people who hold grudges against individuals and, indeed, by ordinary people who, out a misplaced sense of public duty, wrongly report or embellish what they actually saw in order to 'help the police'. Here, the main danger is that their accounts will be accepted uncritically by police officers and set the latter on a wrong track, based on false assumptions, which then places 'blinkers' on the rest of their inquiry.

We shall discuss such problems in relation to major investigations in the next chapter, giving examples of people in the 'drugs world' who were present at or near the scenes of murders and gave evidence that they would otherwise have been reluctant to give, partly because they feared prosecution for drug offences (whether or not the evidence was true is a different question). A related issue – that of the extent to which pressure is put upon people to become *informants* (but not necessarily to give evidence used in court) – will be discussed in Chapter Seven.

Where 'routine' CID work is concerned, there are ample opportunities for officers to put various kinds of pressure on fringe members of criminal groups to give evidence against associates, and witness statements are not infrequently made (and confidential information given) by people who dislike particular suspects. As is the case with pressure on suspects, we have no way of assessing how often such situations obtain, how strong are the pressures applied, nor how often any resulting false witness evidence may, knowingly or unknowingly, be allowed to go forward. The situation is further clouded by a lack of clear guidance on what are the limits of propriety in this area. Nevertheless, we can only conclude that, however honourable officers' intentions (and it may be worth saying that we ourselves are convinced, from long conversations with officers we have known personally for some time, that very few detectives would deliberately manipulate witnesses in order to convict somebody they did not *believe* to be 'guilty'), there is a substantial risk of injustices arising from this source – a risk increased in divisional CID work by the sheer volume of cases to deal with and the consequent lack of time to check information carefully.

One area which we believe deserves attention in this context – and is of relevance to 'honest' as well as to 'malicious' or 'criminal' witnesses – is the standard process by which witness statements are taken. It is rare for witnesses to write these themselves. In general, a police officer will seek to reconstruct what they have said into a more coherent narrative and write it down in their presence, before asking the witness to sign the result. As the detective writes the statement, he or she will run through the victim's or witness's story, frequently checking details and asking them to go over certain parts in their own words, so that these may be noted more accurately. The important point, however, is that the statement is, to a considerable extent, a 'police construction'. It is not the unprompted narrative of the witness, but a carefully crafted summary, often designed, among other things, to establish certain evidential points necessary to meet the technical requirements of proving guilt of a particular criminal offence.

Statement-taking, indeed, is a *skill* which, many senior CID officers told us, is one of the marks of a 'good detective'. It is also one of the products of investigative work in which supervisors tend to take a particular interest, quite often requiring DCs to go back and take further statements when either they, or a uniform officer, have failed to cover all the points needed for them to constitute 'good evidence'. Provided that the witness is given a full opportunity to rephrase anything which does not accord with his or her recollections, the practices described are perfectly justifiable, given the legal requirements and the importance of not burdening the courts with long, rambling and evidentially useless narrative accounts.[16]

Nevertheless, there remains a danger that witnesses may be subtly manipulated into changing their 'story', or persuaded that certain points are irrelevant, so that initial ambiguity or uncertainty are removed and facts relevant to a subsequent defence are not included. An example from a case we observed illustrates the point.

The case involved theft from a car. The victim was driven round the nearby streets to try and locate the suspect. After a short while, a uniform police patrol announced that they had stopped a person fitting the description and asked that the victim be brought to the scene to make an identification. On first seeing the suspect, the victim, who was accompanied by a DC, was hesitant, but then declared that he was 'fairly sure' that this was the person. The DC pressed him, asking him how sure and he increased his assessment to '90 per cent'. When the Detective Constable radioed the station, he stated that the victim was '95 per cent certain' in his identification. In the statement he subsequently took (a

---

[16] It is true that, if the suspect pleads not guilty, his or her lawyer can cross-examine the witness in court. Nevertheless, not only do many people plead guilty faced with apparently damning statement evidence against them, but initial statements tend to become 'set in aspic' and, once signed, make it psychologically difficult for the witness to deviate from them significantly. This makes it extremely important that every effort is made to produce a full and accurate account of their recollections at an early stage.

process not observed by the researcher), the words appeared, 'I am certain that the person . . .'

Subtle pressures and omissions of this kind are of extremely low visibility, and even if supervisors were mindful to prevent them, under present circumstances there is very little they could do. The above points may also be considered within the framework of the argument (put forward most cogently by McConville *et al* 1991) that the police basically adopt a 'crime control', rather than a 'due process' approach to the investigative task and are psychologically geared towards constructing cases against particular suspects they are convinced are guilty, rather than 'seeking the truth' in a totally objective fashion. To the extent that this is correct, there is, in addition to the time factor, the problem that there is little incentive to officers to seek to 'undermine their own case' by questioning 'friendly' witness evidence closely. Beyond this, of course, is the danger that initial mistakes will be compounded by the placing of pressure on other witnesses to make statements supporting the false theory. There are few formal mechanisms in place, and little formal guidance to officers, to counteract the risks in this area.

Police eye-witness accounts

A third potential weak spot in the control of investigations, particularly applicable to divisional CID work (and perhaps even more so to arrests made by uniform PCs) resides in the possibility of police officers 'gilding the lily' in cases in which other evidence is weak, by claiming to have seen suspects take actions which incriminate them. One ex-police officer gave us an example from his time as a uniform PC, when he saw a suspect approach a stolen van containing stolen goods, but then walk away when spotting the officer. He was advised by a detective colleague that, as this was insufficient evidence of involvement, he should state that he saw the person unlock the van door, and also that he should find another officer to claim that he had been with him and seen the same thing. When the PC looked dubious, the detective commented – in a phrase which had stuck in our informant's mind for many years – that 'a good CID officer would be "practical" about it.'

When we discussed these sorts of situations with supervisors, it was clear that none thought there was anything that could be done to prevent them occurring, beyond trying to engender an atmosphere in which ethical behaviour is the norm and DCs are prepared to 'lose' cases in which they know beyond doubt that a person is guilty but the available evidence falls short of that required to get a conviction. The importance of supervisors' attitudes in setting the 'tone' is reinforced by the revelation that the 'colleague' who gave the advice in the above example was a

Detective Sergeant. This little example takes us back again to the central questions of to what extent 'invisible' forms of police activity which may impact upon the quality and fairness of investigations can be controlled through 'supervision' and how, too, it can be ensured that supervisors themselves set the desired standards.

Concluding remarks

Before moving on to look at a different investigative context, it may be helpful to draw together our main arguments and findings to date. Our focus so far, we repeat, has remained primarily (and deliberately) a negative one, with an emphasis upon problems, 'weak spots' and 'worst case scenarios'. We have, however, hinted at ways forward, including through developments currently emerging from within the police service. These will be discussed in more depth in Chapter Eight, which will be devoted to a search for strategies for overcoming the problems we have identified and for examples of 'best practice'.

We have argued that detective work, by its very nature, has always contained the potential for individuals and groups to enter a slippery slope of dubious practice, ranging from general 'sloppiness' in checking facts to deliberate fabrication of evidence. The risk of malpractice – always present merely by virtue of the informal contact with the 'criminal world' which is necessary to do the job effectively – is increased by a combination of factors inherent in the 'CID tradition': the notion of a separate, more attractive and higher status career in an 'elite' department, open only to those who 'earn' it through 'results'; the consequent pressures to make high numbers of 'good arrests' (and the rewards for making them); individualistic, entrepreneurial and secretive workstyles; personalised selection and recruitment processes; the 'charismatic' style of management, based on the assumption that DCs can generally be trusted to work with a minimum of supervision; the confusions in the role of the Detective Sergeant; and the invisibility of much CID activity to outsiders (including uniform colleagues), perpetuated by a close-knit occupational culture.

In the context of the divisional CID office, these problems are exacerbated by the high volume of cases – including some very serious cases – dealt with on their own by officers of the lowest rank; by the practical problems of DSs, themselves burdened by caseloads, in 'keeping tabs on' what DCs are doing; and by the desire of individuals to 'make a mark' in order to establish themselves on the first rung of a career in this specialist department.

At present, the prevention of the serious injustices which can result from both deliberate malpractice and lack of thoroughness in investigations, is heavily dependent upon the personal integrity of CID officers of all ranks, but above all upon the conscientious discharge of the considerable responsibilities falling upon managers and front-line supervisors (many of whom, it should be noted, learned their 'trade' when serving as DCs in the pre-PACE era): this demands the exercise of considerable strength of character, in resisting the temptation to revert to being 'one of the boys', in insisting upon strict adherence to unpopular rules, and in being prepared to 'blow the whistle' when this becomes necessary. As many experienced managers told us, the 'ethos' of a detective unit is set, in the main, not by the DCs, but by the character of the 'moral leadership' provided by those of higher ranks. The major question this raises – to which we shall return in our concluding chapter – is whether a system so dependent upon individual integrity and strength of character is adequate to prevent repetitions of past failings, or whether more formal (or 'bureaucratic') mechanisms of control, less dependent upon the individual, are necessary.

6. HOLMES-Based Major Inquiries

INTRODUCTION

We turn now to the reactive investigation of major crime, in the context of 'teamwork' among structured groups of CID officers. A fair amount of very serious crime, particularly in metropolitan areas, is in fact investigated by individual officers in the ways described in the previous chapter; other major crime is tackled by the proactive 'targeting' of offenders, which we shall discuss in Chapter Seven. Here, however, we are interested in the investigation of single and series offences such as murder, rape and major robberies or assaults, to which the police response has been to set up an 'incident room', often with the aid of the computer-based Home Office (Large) Major Enquiry System (HOLMES).

Decisions as to what size of 'team' to set up, and whether or not to use HOLMES, depend largely on the complexity of the case and whether or not there is a clear suspect. In one force we looked at, there was a standard procedure to be followed by subdivisions as soon as any 'major crime' (a definition of which was given in Force Orders) was reported. This involved contacting the head of the force Serious Crime Squad, who – after familiarising himself with the circumstances – would decide the level at which it should be investigated, ranging from leaving it entirely to the division, through providing some advice and assistance to a divisional team, to the full HOLMES 'treatment'.

The largest force we studied set up 19 HOLMES investigations during 1991, 16 of which involved murder, the other three involving fraud, arson and large-scale burglaries. In another, 11 major incidents were investigated using HOLMES: only four of these were murder inquiries, the other seven involving offences ranging from rape to armed robbery. It must be remembered that these inquiries represent only a tiny fraction of investigations undertaken by a force and, typically, fewer than one in a thousand cases will be investigated using the computer-based system.

Although few in number, investigations under HOLMES tend to be the most complex and challenging cases. In general, they are set up because there is no obvious suspect and, often, only limited initial evidence on which to base the inquiry. Indeed, one senior CID officer remarked that if it were not for their serious nature, many would not have got past any formal crime screening system. Because of this, such investigations are expected to be long-running, taking weeks or months rather than days to complete. Further, once designated as a major inquiry, the investigation will receive generous allocations of personnel, which can involve the commitment of over one hundred officers at any one time and hence place a major drain on force resources.

One consequence of such resourcing and the publicity which often surrounds these investigations is that the inquiry team and, in particular, the Senior Investigating Officer (SIO) come under great pressure to secure a 'result'. There are a number of sources of such pressure.

First, where murders are concerned, forces do not like having unsolved cases on their books. Second, there is a general expectation within the police force that, given sufficient resources, all crime is detectable and that, if the inquiry is run properly, a result should ensue. Third, because major investigations tend to have a high public profile, there is pressure from the media to produce a result and, if one is not forthcoming, questions may be raised about the competence of the inquiry and the SIO (cf., for example, the Julie Dart and Stephanie Slater investigations). There are also other, more subtle, pressures which stem from within the force. News travels fast during investigations and information about recent developments is avidly sought by divisional detectives. Internally, at least, major investigations are conducted in a glare of comment and debate which, as the inquiry drags on, can become increasingly critical. Further, divisional commanders, concerned by the continuing abstractions necessary to staff the inquiry, repeatedly make it clear that they want their officers back as soon as possible. Finally, career detectives can make their names in clearing up major cases. For the SIO, running a successful investigation can be an important step towards advancement up the promotion ladder.

The HOLMES system

In general, HOLMES investigations are housed on the division in which the crime was committed, and headed by the Detective Superintendent or Detective Chief Inspector in charge of the local CID office. (In one of our forces, however, divisions no longer had Detective Superintendents or DCIs, and major inquiries were often run by senior officers from headquarters, one of whose specific jobs was to provide assistance to divisions in such cases). CID officers to staff the inquiry will be drawn from a number of sources – from the 'host' division, through 'mutual aid' from other divisions, and from Central Support Units or Serious Crime Squads, which often provide the key expertise to man and operate the HOLMES computer system itself. Finally, resources may be drawn from Operational Support Groups, which consist of a central reserve of uniformed officers whose main role is to provide support at major public events such as football matches but who, in most forces, also undertake house to house inquiries for major investigations. Major inquiry teams are, therefore, *ad hoc* groupings of officers brought together for a limited period with a single aim.

In the first instance, running a major inquiry is a problem of logistics, of assembling a team, of providing accommodation for the team, of securing the use of vehicles, a communication system and so forth. Because of the size of the inquiry team and the amount of information that it will generate, a central problem is how to coordinate the activities of teams and how to record, and evaluate the significance of, the information that is generated. This is achieved through the use of the HOLMES computer system.

In essence, HOLMES is a computerised information storage and retrieval system which allows for all information emanating from the inquiry to be stored, indexed, cross referenced and interrogated for investigative significance. Formally, there are five major aims of the system:

i. To provide the officer in charge with an accurate record of the state of the inquiry.

ii. To show the state of the inquiry and outstanding work.

iii. To provide the inquiry with an accurate record of all people and vehicles connected with the inquiry.

iv. To record information in a manner which allows suspects to be located.

v. To provide a record to aid legal decision making.

However, the HOLMES system is not just a computer system but is also accompanied by a set of standardised procedures (Major Incident Room Standard Administration Procedures) which govern the input, processing and accessing of data, the day to day running of the incident room, the allocation of work and the review of information within the system. In essence, it provides a support service for the SIO, although it is important to note that he or she is not part of the HOLMES team and, indeed, along with most other senior officers, does not normally have direct access to their computer. Only authorised users – people who have undergone HOLMES training and have their own entry password – can input and retrieve data. Although not specifically designed as a safeguard against misconduct, this rule creates a formal separation between investigation managers and system operators which can be valuable in demonstrating the integrity of the system.

HOLMES inquiry teams display the standard features of bureaucratic organisation and control, thus standing in strong contrast to normal patterns of investigation on divisions. There is a clear division of labour and specialisation of function within the inquiry team, which divides into three broad areas: first, the HOLMES administrative team, second, the HOLMES investigative team and finally, the outside inquiry teams. Above these three groups is the SIO and his or her deputy.

The HOLMES administrative team is headed by an Office Manager, who is normally a Detective Inspector, supported by an administrative officer who should be a uniform Inspector. The Office Manager has the role of managing the logistical problems of the inquiry. In the first instance, he or she is responsible for setting up the office, ensuring adequate accommodation, providing communication equipment and vehicles, and so on. Once the investigation is underway, the Office Manager is responsible for managing the rostering arrangements, overtime budget, welfare and any matters relating to equipment, accommodation or personnel that may arise. Finally, the Office Manager is responsible for keeping the Policy Book, which provides a formal record of the key investigative decisions taken by the inquiry team.

The investigative side to the HOLMES system revolves around five key roles: Receiver, Indexer, Statement Reader, Action Allocator and Exhibits Officer. All personnel having access to the HOLMES system receive basic training, generally a one week course, in the principles and practices of the system. In addition, officers for the roles of Statement Readers and Indexers receive prolonged specialist training.

The Receiver is responsible for the immediate review of all the information that comes into the system and determines whether urgent action is required. The Receiver will also set the priorities for information to be entered into the system (which can quickly develop backlogs of documents awaiting input) and keep the SIO informed of any important developments. The Statement Reader's job, as the name implies, is to review all statements entering the system and to determine any follow-up actions necessitated by information contained within the statements. The Indexer's job, which is performed by civilians in some forces, is to read all statements and, using a standardised procedure, index all the relevant points so that key words (eg names, addresses, vehicles) can be cross referenced within the system. The Action Allocator's job is to distribute work to the outside inquiry teams and to ensure that the work is carried out and the result entered into the system. The Action Allocator also determines the time frame within which tasks should be completed. Each action is entered into the system and allocated a number of days for completion. The system will flag any actions not completed within the given period. The Exhibits Officer is responsible for the logging, storage and retrieval of all exhibits which may be needed in evidence or required for forensic examination, eg original statements, property, clothing, specialist reports.

This role separation and division of labour creates clear lines of responsibility and accountability and provides a detailed system for reviewing the quality and importance of the information entering the system.[1]

Statements from witnesses (in the broadest sense of the term) form one of the main categories of the records stored in the HOLMES database. The other key records are Personal Descriptor Forms (PDF), Vehicle Descriptor Forms and Officer Message Forms. At the initial stage of the inquiry, where there is no clear suspect, PDFs are filled out for all persons contacted in the course of the inquiry. They provide a detailed physical description of these persons, their addresses and the vehicles they use, as well as details of their relatives, friends and associates. As the inquiry progresses and, for example, it becomes clear that the offender being sought has certain traits, more limited parameters may be set before PDFs are completed. Finally, miscellaneous information may be placed on the system at the behest of officers involved in the inquiry. For instance, anonymous telephone calls purporting to give information, or information

---

[1] To give a clearer picture of how the system works in practice, it is worth considering a concrete example:

> A statement is taken by an officer from a witness at the scene of a murder. In the statement, among other things, the witness describes seeing a "W reg Austin Metro" leaving the area shortly after the murder. If this has not already been picked up by the Receiver, the Statement Reader will decide that the vehicle should be traced and the owner interviewed and will, therefore, raise an 'action'. The Action Allocator assigns the job to a pair of detectives and specifies how long the action may remain open. If the action has not been cleared within the stated time, he or she will chase up the officers concerned for a progress report. Let us suppose that after three days the officers from the outside inquiry team succeed in tracing the owner of the vehicle and taking a statement. This statement will first be reviewed by the Receiver, who will determine if an urgent action is required as a result of the new information. The statement will then be typed into the system and typed copies passed to the Statement Reader and Indexer. The Statement Reader will go through the statement line by line to determine if any actions should be raised. Such actions could include interviewing any persons named in the statement in order to provide corroboration of the person's story. If an action is raised, the Action Allocator will assign this action to an inquiry team, and so the process continues. The Indexer, meanwhile, will index all the information contained within the statement so that it can be cross referenced with other statements and information already entered in the system.

provided by people who refuse to make a formal statement, can be entered via Officer Message Forms.

The outside inquiry teams are usually made up of paired detectives and are assigned specific elements of the investigation. Outside inquiry teams could include a 'background inquiry team', whose job it is to find out as much as possible about the victim, or a 'family team', whose brief is to liaise with the victim's family and deduce any information relevant to the inquiry. Specialist inquiry teams may also be set up to follow specific lines of inquiry. For instance, in one investigation, a 'prostitute squad' of over 40 detectives under the command of an Acting Detective Inspector was established to trace and interview the 300 prostitutes who worked in a particular locality. A database was compiled from all existing police sources and a questionnaire devised to be administered to all known prostitutes. The aim of the questionnaire was to determine any knowledge of the victim, full details of each woman's whereabouts at the time of the murder, whether they had been into the victim's house, and so on. Each prostitute interviewed had a detailed PDF filled in on her. In addition, all prostitutes found on the street were questioned to ensure that their names were included on the list. It is important to note that outside inquiry teams have clear terms of reference and standardised procedures. The teams are also task based and each task comprises only a small part of the whole investigation. Thus, rather than embodying the entrepreneurial, individualistic detective style found on division, the outside inquiry teams in major investigations are more akin to piece workers, operating within fixed parameters and with limited discretion.

Again in contrast to divisional work, the SIO, apart from the initial stages of the inquiry where he or she will attend the scene and the *post mortem*, does not play a 'hands-on' investigative role, but is largely office bound and responsible for the overall management of the investigation. The SIO's role is, essentially, that of chief policy maker, and includes setting the long term parameters and direction of the inquiry. However, while the HOLMES system itself generates actions and routine lines of inquiry in accordance with the overall parameters set by the SIO, there are still day to day decisions to be taken about priorities and redirecting resources as new information comes to light.

Owing to the division of labour and the fragmented nature of inquiries, it is extremely important that at least one person – first and foremost, the SIO – has, at any one time, a complete overview of the investigation. The role of SIO is consequently very demanding, both physically and mentally. Officers in this position frequently work 12–14 hour days, seven days a week. They are responsible for conducting the daily or, in many cases, twice daily briefings of the inquiry teams to ensure that everyone involved is aware of current developments and to appraise headquarters of the current state of play.

'Weak spots' and safeguards

Despite the impressive organisational structure and cross-checking systems apparent from the above description, it should not be assumed that HOLMES inquiries are immune from weaknesses, errors or even malpractice. The familiar doubts and problems surrounding the reliability of confession evidence and the veracity of witness statements do not disappear simply because the statements are fed into a computer, nor are the potential misjudgements, prejudices and human frailties of investigators eliminated.

A particular problem area which stood out in four of the murder investigations we discussed with officers, was that of unreliable witnesses. Three of these cases involved 'drug world' murders, in which several drug addicts had been present at or near the scene of the murder. Several of these either told blatant lies or were very reluctant to make any statement at all. In one case, a senior officer told us that 'quite a lot of pressure' (on which he did not elaborate) had been put on the group to make witness statements, which became important to the resulting case. Although quite sure of the basic sequence of events and of the guilt of the suspect, he admitted that he was still unsure of the truth of some of these statements. The HOLMES system, he recognised, could not guarantee that investigations were not sent on false trails by misinformation, nor that the 'pressure' put on people to produce information was within acceptable limits. In the final analysis, these were matters of personal judgement in a difficult and uncertain area, which could ultimately, if bad decisions were taken, result in a wrongful conviction and 'the wheel coming off' for the team.

Nevertheless, as this officer and many others pointed out, there are a number of distinct features, both in the external controls provided by PACE and within the inquiry system itself, which limit the chances of serious procedural errors, police malpractice, or acceptance at face value of false witness or confession evidence. These safeguards can be broken down into five broad areas, on which we shall comment in turn: i. PACE, ii. Systemised review procedures, iii. Open and accountable decision-making, iv. Separation of managerial and quality control functions from investigative functions, v. Clear and comprehensive documentation of the investigation.

PACE

As with all police investigations, major inquiries are regulated by the provisions of the Police and Criminal Evidence Act and the codes of conduct governing its implementation. According to many senior detectives, it is in major inquiries that PACE has had the greatest impact, because it was here that investigations were previously afforded the greatest license. PACE, by providing independent regulation of the conditions and duration of custody, increasing access to solicitors and introducing the tape recording of interviews, has significantly reduced the opportunities for detectives to place pressure on a suspect or a community for information or admissions. Strategies such as blanket arrests of active criminals to uncover information, 'hostage taking' (the arrest of members of suspects' families) and falsifying interview records have, through PACE, been largely eradicated. While some of these changes have been accepted and even welcomed by many of the senior officers we spoke to, we also found a considerable degree of dissatisfaction and frustration. The general view expressed was that 'the pendulum has swung too far in the wrong direction', or that 'we are now acting with both hands tied behind our backs.'

Criticism was centred upon the interrelated issues of the 'right of silence' and the restrictions imposed by PACE. Procedurally, the conduct of major investigations comes closest, among all investigative methods in use, to a model of inquisitorial truth finding, since the system is designed, and resources are allocated, to enable the systematic cross checking and corroboration of all evidence. It is in this context that the almost universal police criticism of the 'right of silence' has to be understood. The overwhelming view expressed to us was that the safeguards in PACE, particularly the access to a solicitor, have made this right an 'anachronism'. Silence, or the refusal to answer certain questions, they argued, should be allowed to be commented upon in court as a possible indication of guilt. The innocent, it was claimed many times, have nothing to fear from cooperation. In addition, the exercise of the right of silence was seen as hindering the 'search for the truth' and could even rebound on the person exercising it. For instance, one DCI argued that, in cases where there is evidence to link a person to the scene of a crime, if that person does not disclose the presence of others at the scene, who may be more culpable, the investigation may be led along a false trail and could even end in mistaken charges against him or her.

From the SIO's point of view, the inquisitorial nature of the investigation is further undermined, once a suspect has been arrested, by the rules governing the length of detention, which can create a 'race against the clock'. Where a person in custody, for instance, puts forward a possible alibi or makes claims about the involvement of others, the limits on detention provide little time to conduct the necessary inquiries to test these claims, arrange identification parades, have forensic tests carried out, and so on. (It was partly for this reason that one force had installed facilities enabling other officers to listen in on interviews – follow up inquiries could then commence immediately.) This is compounded by the fact that, in practice, twenty four hours detention does not mean twenty four hours of interviewing, due to refreshment periods, rest periods, the necessity of waiting for solicitors and the requirement for the suspect to receive eight hours uninterrupted sleep. In reality, therefore, twenty four hours detention can be whittled down to five or six hours of interview time. In one case we examined, for instance, the suspect who was finally charged was held for 52 hours and, although the whole investigation centred around the information emanating from the interviews, only 12 hours of interviews were actually conducted. While suspects can, of course, be released on police bail pending further inquiries, officers were reluctant to release people they considered either dangerous or likely to disappear.

Despite these pressures on the investigation, and the fact that PACE rules were seen to place unfair restrictions on the inquiry, our observations and interviews suggested that senior officers were not prepared to risk compromising the investigation – and, ultimately, 'losing' the case – by breaching the rules. The certainty of detailed scrutiny in these important cases was regarded as making scrupulous compliance essential. Indeed, although the presence of solicitors was generally seen as a hindrance to the investigation, the importance of avoiding later allegations that an interview had been oppressive, led most SIOs to insist that no interview should be conducted without a solicitor present.

For instance, in one case we observed, a person who had been arrested during a HOLMES murder inquiry for subsidiary offences of theft, declined his right to have a solicitor present. At this stage, it was not believed that he had played a part in the murder. However, as soon as it became apparent that he may have been substantially involved, the interview was stopped, he was re-arrested on suspicion of murder, and the SIO insisted that a solicitor be called.

It should also be noted that, in these long periods of detention, custody officers and uniform duty inspectors change shifts, and the uniform divisional superintendent often keeps in touch with what is happening, so there is some oversight of the general treatment of the suspect from several middle-ranking officers not involved in the investigation.

Finally, a particular idea which appeared to us to be sensible in this context – which was being seriously considered in one of the forces we looked at – was that of appointing a 'PACE Officer' to each major inquiry team. This would be a sort of 'super custody officer' whose sole responsibility would be to advise the team on any developments which might be challenged as incompatible with PACE, or, more broadly, any police actions which might later be vulnerable to defence challenge.

Systematic review procedures

As described earlier, the 'legwork' in HOLMES investigations is carried out by large numbers of CID officers, who are formally allocated specific tasks (or 'actions') to complete: principally, obtaining statements from, or cross-checking information about, people whose names have cropped up during the inquiry. As in divisional CID work, the manner in which DCs carry out these tasks is largely invisible to senior officers – a situation which, we have pointed out, contains some risk of producing unreliable evidence. However, in the context of HOLMES inquiries, these risks are minimised. First of all, there is little incentive for junior officers to manipulate witnesses or to fabricate evidence and, even if they did so, there would be a high chance of it being discovered. The situation is quite different, in that:

i. Whereas divisional CID officers usually carry out all the different elements of an inquiry themselves, here they are dealing with only one small part of the whole.

ii. Unlike in routine investigations, where the quality of their 'paperwork' may hardly be monitored in many cases, here it is subject to close scrutiny by the Statement Reader, the Indexer, and, if significant, the SIO.

iii. Whereas any cross-checking or corroboration of evidence in routine inquiries is undertaken by the same officer, here each significant piece of information is subject not only to cross-checking against other information already in the computer, but to a follow up inquiry which is likely to be carried out by another detective. Hence any major discrepancies are highly likely to be discovered.

These systematic review and cross-checking procedures also provide some safeguard against the possibility of false or malicious evidence from victims and witnesses being accepted at face value because they are convenient to the inquiry.

The upshot of this discussion is, that if one is looking for 'weak spots', in the sense of risks of major errors, oppressive conduct, concealment of 'inconvenient' evidence, or fabrication of 'helpful' evidence, it is unlikely that they will be found in the activities of junior officers seconded to the inquiry. One would have to look instead at the person or small team at the head of the inquiry.

As we have said, there are major pressures on the SIO to produce a 'result' and the possibility has to be faced that he or she might try to build a case against a suspect on dubious or improperly obtained evidence or to conceal evidence helpful to the defence. However, there are further monitoring procedures which minimise the chances of this happening. In some forces, the headquarters-based HOLMES team is responsible not only for setting up the system and providing technical assistance, but has a specific 'quality control' function. This includes randomly selecting statements and tracing them through the system, checking to ensure proper indexing has been completed and relevant actions allocated. Many forces now also have the formal requirement of an internal review by a senior officer (sometimes from another force) independent of the investigation team, once cases have run for a given period (often, six weeks) without resolution. This can include quality checks of the above kind, together with an overall review of the progress of the investigation and its main lines of inquiry. Although such reviews are primarily concerned with questions of efficiency and effectiveness – and although criticisms were heard in one force of a tendency to appoint reviewing officers personally acquainted with the SIO – they have the additional effect of providing an incentive towards integrity and good practice. Finally, it should be remembered that SIOs do not normally have direct access to the computer system, so it would be difficult for them, should they be so tempted, to tamper with any entries already made.

Open and accountable decision-making

In spite of the traditional tendency for detectives to adopt an individualistic and secretive approach to investigations, the progress and direction of major inquiries, internally at least, is often a very open affair, with inputs from many different people. Although the SIO has the final responsibility for decision making, he or she is supported by a policy team. The policy team consists of the SIO, the Deputy SIO, the Office Manager, Receiver, Action Allocator and the head of the outside inquiry teams. In general, the policy team meets each morning to update the SIO and each other on the previous 24 hours' developments and to agree the priorities for the next 24 hours. Although we only had access to only two such meetings and cannot generalise, it was clear that, in these inquiries at least, the atmosphere encouraged a free exchange of information, ideas and suggestions of possible avenues to explore: it was not held simply to provide ratification of the SIO's decisions. As far as the SIOs were concerned, the policy team was an open forum, all information was shared and nothing was held back. The decision making was subject to internal scrutiny and to challenge.

One senior officer told us that in several murder inquiries he had worked on, the policy team had not been in unanimous agreement that the person finally charged was responsible. While some may see this as potentially unnerving, it demonstrates a healthy critical edge which ensures that all possibilities are considered. The policy team represents an important check against inquiries becoming 'blinkered' or 'single track', as well as providing a forum where doubts can be raised.

On the other hand, other officers told us of HOLMES cases in which the SIO had acted in an 'autocratic' manner and had discouraged criticism of his decisions and beliefs about the guilt of particular suspects. This approach was said to be becoming less common – a 'hangover' from the days when, as one DCI put it, one senior detective 'carried the whole case in his head' and saw his team as 'an extension of his own ego'. Such an approach was associated with individual 'glory-seeking', as illustrated by the desire of the 'boss' to carry out the key interviews and personally to read out the charges at the end of the investigation. These attitudes and practices, it was said many times, are dying out and 'modern' SIOs tend to see themselves as 'professional managers' rather than 'bosses', ie as coordinators of a complex organisational process rather than as inspirational leaders cracking crime through following their own instincts. Certainly, although we can only give our own impressions, this was that the cases we observed were managed very much in the 'new style'.

A further important feature of major inquiries – which symbolises the 'new approach' we have been describing – is the Policy Book. In this book, which is also logged as a computer file, a record is kept of all the major decisions taken in an inquiry: for instance, the parameters of house to house inquiries, which lines of investigation should be pursued and why, and the decision to arrest and question a suspect. The Policy Book, therefore, becomes a chronological record of the progress of the investigation which is open to scrutiny, particularly by senior officers at headquarters. As one Chief Superintendent explained, initially the introduction of the Policy Book was viewed with great suspicion by SIO's, who 'thought it would be used to hammer them into the ground when the inquiry went wrong'. He stressed that this was not the case, but that the existence of the Policy Book made the SIOs think more carefully about their decisions and the justifications for them. If the decisions turned out to be wrong, as long as the justification was rational there was no cause for recriminations.

Finally, we were made aware of another important trend in major inquiries which is relevant to external scrutiny: the involvement of the Crown Prosecution Service at an early stage. It is now almost common practice in some forces, once a suspect in a major inquiry has been arrested and interviewed, to discuss the status and strength of the evidence with a senior member of the local CPS and to ask advice on whether there is sufficient to charge or whether any areas need to be strengthened. Members of the CPS to whom we spoke informally on this subject generally welcomed the trend, although some concerns were expressed about the dangers of blurring of roles and compromising of the CPS's independence. Our police interviewees had no doubts at all about its value, in terms of saving wasted effort as well as receiving the benefit of expert legal advice.

In sum, while the combination of the policy team, the Policy Book, regular reviews, briefings and the involvement of the CPS, does not in itself guarantee the integrity of the inquiry, it does provide a medium for peer review and challenge which facilitates keeping all lines of inquiry open and guards against premature closure on a weak case. Further, because of the fairly open nature of these systems, individual malpractice is made very much less likely.

Separation of managerial and quality control functions from investigative functions

One of the greatest safeguards of the system, if operated successfully, lies in the clear separation of administrative, investigative and 'quality control' functions. We have already mentioned many of the ways in which this occurs, but they bear brief repetition to bring out the key points.

i. Although SIOs have by far the most demanding job, the fact that they do not carry out day-to-day inquiry tasks means that they are able to maintain a 'distance' from the investigation and, hence, to concentrate on strategic decision making. One constant theme reiterated in interviews with SIOs was the necessity of 'keeping an open mind', i.e. not prematurely closing down options or becoming blinkered to certain courses of action. However, this is easier said than done. One strategy that SIOs can employ to prevent themselves becoming committed to one version of events is to avoid becoming involved in interviewing victims, witnesses or suspects. (It is also worth noting, in passing, that senior officers, who have been 'tied to the office' for many years, may not make the best interviewers – this task is better given to, say, a DS who is interviewing almost daily.)

ii. The HOLMES system, although central to the investigation, is also, in another sense, separated from it. Few SIOs are trained in the technical side of the system and therefore most are not authorised to input information into the computer or to access data themselves. The SIO is therefore reliant upon the HOLMES teams to record and provide information.

iii. The roles of Indexer and Statement Reader, although not designed to prevent procedural impropriety or malpractice, do provide an independent source of review, or 'quality control', of all information within the system. Evidence which is either inconvenient or suggests other lines of inquiry cannot easily be kept hidden and should come to light through routine procedures. This process is also facilitated by the analytical capabilities of the HOLMES system. The system is able to generate 'sequence of events' logs by using the indices and cross references created by the Indexer. The Sequence of Events (SOE) file draws on all information held within the system and does not differentiate between evidence which is and is not convenient to the building of a case against an accused. For instance, if one witness claimed that a suspect had been present at the scene, a sequence of events file would immediately indicate who else was present, and checks could be made to see whether this information could be corroborated.

iv. The periodic involvement of headquarters CID staff, including the head of CID, also provides a useful quality control check. Through review of the Policy Book, regular updates by telephone and visits to the inquiry teams, senior officers can maintain an oversight of the direction of the inquiry whilst not becoming involved themselves.

Documentation of the inquiry

The final area in major investigations which stands in clear contrast to divisional CID work, is that the system contains an entire record of the investigation. Every item relevant to the inquiry will either be logged in the system, as in the case of exhibits, or actually contained within the system, as in the case of statements or transcripts of interviews. Such comprehensive record keeping means that the chances of an oversight or malpractice leading to non-disclosure of crucial evidence are minimised. Further, as all documentation is held on a database, it would be difficult technically to tamper with the system to delete statements, or even parts of statements, and leave no trace.

Finally, too, the HOLMES system offers hope of solution to the problem of the disclosure of evidence to the defence after charges have been laid, an issue which has loomed large in several recent 'miscarriage' cases and is still a matter of controversy, particularly since the Saunders ruling. The most common practice in the forces we looked at was to make available to the defence, via the CPS, all 'used' evidence arising from the investigation, together with a list from the database of the names of all other persons who had provided 'unused' statements: they could then request further details if they wished. Some officers also thought it possible, in future, to allow the defence access to the database itself, through the intermediary of HOLMES-trained officers. There is, of course, a possibility that some information will not be entered. This already occurs sometimes for perfectly valid reasons: in one murder case, for example, subsidiary enquiries involving drug dealing were undertaken in parallel with the hunt for the murderer, and not all information relating to these was entered in the system. However, to engage dishonestly in deliberate omission of material evidence would be a risky course for any officer to take. Not only might loose ends be noticed subsequently through cross-checking of other entries, but it would be difficult to achieve without the knowledge and collaboration of other officers in the team. Moreover, it is not always easy at the evidence gathering stage to identify which specific pieces of evidence which are going to be helpful to the defence and, as noted above, once entered, material is very difficult to remove without trace.

To sum up, the pressures on major inquiry teams, and especially on the SIO, can be intense: not only are the cases often extremely complex and difficult (and sometimes involve crimes, such as child murder, which arouse deep emotions), but there can be substantial media interest and concern from force managers about the scale and expense of the inquiry. In the past, such cases were often run in an autocratic, idiosyncratic and 'hands on' manner by a senior detective, with few formal mechanisms for others to review the appropriateness of the lines of inquiry adopted or to question the methods used. While by no means eliminating problems caused by human fallibility, the HOLMES-based inquiry system encourages a much more thorough, professional and rational approach to major investigations, with inbuilt checks and balances. In particular, it provides comprehensive storage and retrieval of evidential material, systematic cross-checking of information, clear divisions of responsibility within the team and regular reviews of the overall direction of the investigation.

7. OFFENDER CENTRED POLICING: REGIONAL CRIME SQUADS AND FORCE DRUGS SQUADS

As noted earlier, there are only limited opportunities for 'proactive' or 'offender centred' operations at divisional level and the majority of investigations are 'reactive' or 'offence centred'. Many force based squads, too, operate primarily in a reactive mode – notably Fraud Squads, Child Abuse Units and, increasingly, Serious Crime Squads or their equivalent. (The latter often retain a proactive brief, but it tends to take second place to supporting divisional officers in investigations of murders and other major recorded offences: outside London there are now very few force squads engaged primarily in targetting major burglars and robbers.)[1] The main site of offender centred investigation is in force-level Drugs Squads and Regional Crime Squads (RCS), although there are smaller units, such as Vehicle Crime Squads and Vice Squads, which also work predominantly in a proactive mode.

Target operations: introductory remarks

Drug investigations epitomize the offender centred approach. Unlike the vast majority of CID work, which arises from specific crime complaints, they are initiated in most cases by police officers acting upon pieces of information offered by, or elicited from, 'informants' on a confidential basis, and sometimes as a result of the observations of officers themselves (such as noting that a particular house is receiving frequent visits from known drug addicts). Such information produces a possible 'target' offender, who becomes the focus of further investigation.

Another feature of drug investigations is that the amount of evidence required to sustain a conviction for possession of controlled drugs is substantially less than in many other types of crime. Once it has been established that drugs were found in a person's possession, no further proof is necessary. The offence of theft, by contrast, requires intent

---

[1] In fact, according to information we obtained from HMCIC's Office, there were only two squads left with the name 'Serious Crime Squad'. Most forces now have 'Crime Support Units', whose main function is to assist divisions with major enquiries. Only a handful had burglary squads.

to be established and proof that the goods in question were actually stolen.

However, while it is relatively easy to obtain the evidence for a successful prosecution for 'possession', it is far more difficult to build a case of 'possession with intent to supply' or 'unlawful supply': in short, prosecuting drug users is easy, obtaining evidence to convict drug dealers is much harder. For instance, anyone arrested in possession of four ounces of cannabis may claim in their defence that they were 'keeping it safe' for someone else, that the drug was for their own personal consumption, that they knew nothing about the drug, or they may refuse to say anything at all. The fact of possessing this amount of the drug would certainly be enough to ensure a conviction for possession, but not necessarily of 'supply'. Drug dealers are well aware of this and are likely, therefore, to admit to the former but not to the latter – a much more serious offence which carries a lengthy prison sentence. To build a case against a drug dealer thus necessitates producing a mosaic of evidence which links the person to both the drug and to the activity of supplying it to others and, ideally, is centred upon catching the dealer 'red handed' in possession of a quantity which could not be ascribed to personal consumption.

Regional Crime Squads also engage in a large (and increasing)[2] number of anti-drugs operations, but their investigations of non drug crime also mirror many of the features described above. The RCS is primarily concerned with the investigation of serious and continuing criminal activity which crosses force boundaries. Although the Squad may look for patterns or series of offences indicating the work of a major criminal or group of criminals, its starting point is usually information through intelligence that particular named individuals are currently 'active' and operating over a wide area: this may or may not tie them to specific past crimes. As with drug inquiries, intelligence and evidence are gathered through the coordinated use of surveillance and informants, the central aim being to catch offenders 'red handed' in the commission of one offence, and, if possible, to generate evidence linking them to a series of offences. Before we deal in more detail with each of the main elements of offender centred investigation – intelligence, surveillance, and informants – it is necessary to document the organisational context in which these investigations take place.

---

[2] This was very clear in one of the RCS we visited, where, although there was a dedicated RCS drugs wing and the forces had their own drug squads, the remaining RCS teams also frequently engaged in drugs-related operations. It was explained that much serious crime is now drug-related and that many 'ex-robbers' are moving into the drug-dealing arena.

Organisational features

Regional Crime Squads

The nine Regional Crime Squads in England and Wales came into formal existence on April 1st, 1965. As the name suggests, a regional crime squad has territorial responsibility which transcends force boundaries and is staffed by detectives from a number of adjacent police forces. The constituent forces of each region provide around 1.25 per cent of their establishment on secondment to their regional Squad. In all, there are about 1,200 detectives seconded to the RCS at any one time, some 230 of whom are deployed in dedicated Drugs Wings. The current terms of reference governing the RCS are set out in Home Office Circular No.28/1987, as follows:

i) to identify and arrest those responsible for serious criminal offences which transcend force and regional boundaries

ii) to cooperate with regional criminal intelligence offices in the generating of intelligence; and

iii) at the request of the chief officers to assist in the investigation of serious crime by undertaking, normally for a limited period, specific tasks agreed with the Regional Coordinator for which the special skills, training and knowledge of experienced Crime Squad officers are especially suited and which are not readily available from other sources.

There are complex special arrangements to secure the accountability of Regional Crime Squads, necessitated by two features. First, its activities cross the boundaries of normal lines of accountability; second, the RCS has no statutory basis, having been set up under Section 13 of the 1964 Police Act as a voluntary collaborative agreement between constituent forces. In theory at least, a Police Authority could withdraw from the arrangement. Each region is headed by a Regional Coordinator, of Detective Chief Superintendent rank, who is accountable to the Chief Constables' Management Committee (CCMC), comprising the Chief Constables of each constituent force and a representative of Her Majesty's Inspectorate of Constabulary. This committee appoints the Regional Coordinator, determines the organisation of the squad, advises the various police authorities on funding, and reports to them on the work of the squad. While the local authorities (together with the CCMC) have a general responsibility for establishment, funding and equipment, as well as for the conduct of RCS operations within their territorial boundaries, day to day control of operations is under the direction of the Regional Coordinator.

The regional coordinators also consult regularly on policy and operations with the national Executive Coordinator, based in the Home Office, an appointee of the Standing Committee of Chief Officers. Strictly speaking, the Executive Coordinator, whose main role is 'to give advice and assistance on all matters to regional crime squads', has no formal powers to direct policy or operations. In reality, however, this advice is seldom ignored.

The basic unit of operation of the Regional Crime Squad is the syndicate. Each syndicate is headed by a Detective Inspector, and comprises 12 officers, who normally work in three teams of four, each team consisting of a Detective Sergeant and three Detective Constables. Syndicates operate out of branch offices, which are located in police stations throughout the region. Each branch office is headed by a Detective Chief Inspector who is the Branch Commander. Branches may have more than one syndicate. Each branch reports to a Detective Superintendent of Operations, who in turn reports to the Regional Coordinator.

Force Drugs Squads

Every force has a dedicated Drugs Squad, which range in size from four to thirty-nine officers. They also display considerable organisational variety. They may be housed at headquarters or in divisional stations, are headed by officers of varying ranks and are under varying degrees of central control. Most, however, are headed by a Detective Inspector who reports through the headquarters CID chain of command. This applied to both squads we looked at, which were based in premises attached to divisional stations.

Most squads appear to have only vague terms of reference.[3] In one of those we visited, the DI had not been issued with any, nor was he aware of any formal job description. The only written statement as to the aims and objectives of his squad was to be found in Force Orders and consisted of little more than a paragraph which was out of date and, as far as the DI was concerned, had little current relevance.

In the absence of explicit terms of reference, it is left very much to the officer in charge to determine the precise objectives of each squad and the style of operation. Such decisions are partly dependent on the size of the unit and the technology and equipment available. Full-scale targetting operations only become feasible as the dominant mode of operation if there are sufficient personnel trained in mobile surveillance techniques,

---

[3] See Wright and Waymont (1992).

and sufficient vehicles, surveillance equipment and dedicated covert and encrypted communications systems.

The squad at which we looked most closely was headed by a Detective Inspector, under whom were six detective sergeants and twelve detective constables. In theory, then, there was a very high supervisory ratio of Sergeants to Constables. However, in practice this was diluted by the organisation of the unit. There were basically three teams, each constituting a DS and four DCs. Of the other three detective sergeants, two were permanently assigned to maintain the chemist register, and one was the unit's financial investigator, whose task it is to trace and seize assets from arrested suppliers.

Investigative Strategies

As already outlined, offender centred investigation has three distinctive features: it is intelligence driven, informant based and surveillance centred. We now examine each of these in more detail.

Intelligence

Whilst divisional CID work is dominated by the requirement to react to crime reports, in the RCS the primary organisational currency is the *intelligence report*. Intelligence reports are centred upon information relating to known offenders and include information such as recent sightings, names of current associates, addresses and vehicles they are using, and so on. This information may emanate from a myriad of police and non-police sources and is collated and held by different intelligence bureaux at force, regional or national level: the Force Intelligence Bureau (FIB), Regional Crime Intelligence Office (RCIO), or National Drugs Intelligence Unit (NDIU), respectively. At the lowest level, the FIB collates all intelligence reports generated at force level and inputted by uniform and CID officers. Intelligence which may have regional or national significance is passed on to the RCIO or NDIU, who evaluate whether it is of the right level to be handled by their systems. For instance, information on street level drug dealers is likely to be of great significance for force Drugs and Vice Squads, but to be deemed unsuitable for inclusion in regional or national intelligence files. Regardless of the level at which organisational collation takes place, all intelligence offices treat information in much the same way, assessing it in respect of its source and reliability before adding it to the relevant computer or manual record.

Although these intelligence reports form the basic raw material for RCS operations, it must be stressed that their volume, diversity and differential quality, together with the uncoordinated nature of inputs which are emanating almost at random from numerous sources, make them only a starting point. Both limited resources and the organisational mandate to concentrate on serious cross border crime mean that only a small minority of reports are considered as possible bases for operations. The most promising of these are worked up by Regional Crime Intelligence Officers (RCIOs), through research and coordination of material, into summary reports known as 'packages'. If thought suitable, these may be nominated for adoption as the basis of full-scale *Target Investigations*, the operations which constitute the main distinguishing feature of the RCS. The process of adoption is formalised and bureaucratic, involving the completion of a comprehensive target nomination form and the submission of full supporting documentation. Nominations emanating from the branch office which are being proposed as full Target Investigations are first vetted by the Branch Commander, one of whom described his role in the following terms:

> 'I suppose I'm a filter. The teams will have worked the information up and submitted through their DI's and I will evaluate on a number of criteria – is it serious enough, is it serial, involving more than one offence, and does it involve travelling criminals'.

The final decision as to whether the package is adopted and thus allocated intensive resources is taken by the Regional Coordinator.

The importance of this process is that the selection and allocation of major targets is rational and scrutinised. Not only does this ensure that the RCS is focussing its attention on the right level and type of criminal activity, but it also means that the quality of the initial intelligence is reviewed: that information which might be of dubious veracity or malicious intent is properly researched, evaluated and confirmed before embarking upon a lengthy process of evidence gathering directed towards the arrest of the 'target'. Thus although the process is clearly that of 'case construction' (McConville *et al* 1991), in the sense that guilt is assumed before the investigation proper begins, the chances of a case being prepared on the basis of erroneous suspicions are low.

The processing and use of intelligence in the force Drugs Squads was found to be far less systematic, less monitored and subject to fewer bureaucratic forms of control. There are three reasons for this. First, practically every 'job' emanates from within the squad; second, the work does not usually involve the coordination of inquiries and operations across force or regional boundaries; and finally, Drugs Squad detectives operate much more than RCS officers as individualistic 'intelligence entrepreneurs'. Some intelligence was said to be kept secret even from office colleagues, while most officers were very reluctant to commit it to intelligence reports which would have a wider circulation. One reason for this reluctance in one force was a generally held belief that the Drugs Wing of the Regional Crime Squad would 'steal' their intelligence, use it to run their own operations and then take all the credit. It was particularly resented, for instance, that the Drugs Wing had free access to Force Intelligence but that this was not reciprocated by giving them open access to Regional intelligence files.

Within Drugs Squads there are often two competing styles of operation, which may exist in tandem. One is for the squad to operate primarily on short term limited objectives aimed at producing a high number of arrests, generally being content with 'possession' charges. Some officers were critical of the somewhat opportunisitic and unplanned nature of these operations, calling them 'smash and grab' or 'kick it and see' jobs. This style of work was seen as related to concerns to 'keep up the figures' and as a sign that the force hierarchy was less interested in the quality of arrests than in their quantity.

The second broad style is closer to that of the RCS, exhibiting a more systematic use of intelligence, both in selecting targets and in generating evidence to sustain charges of 'supply' against dealers higher up the distribution chain. Although the 'numbers game' was still seen as dominant, there were signs in both the Drugs Squads we visited of a policy shift in the direction of this latter style. In one squad, the shift was quite marked: first, because of the recent acquisition of a fleet of well-equipped dedicated surveillance vehicles and, second, because the Drugs Squad was under the direction of a new DI who was familiar with RCS practices. Thus, each of the three teams had been assigned one 'major target' operation and two or three subsidiary targets. The major target operations were subject to procedures similar to those deployed in the RCS, requiring the completion of a detailed target nomination form and vetting by the Detective Inspector as to operational feasibility and the importance of the target. In addition, these target operations were logged at headquarters with the Superintendent in charge of Squads. It is important to recognize that in smaller Drugs Squads, without such equipment and RCS experience, intelligence will almost inevitably remain less systematised and less subject to review. However, the use of intelligence is so important to Drugs Squads that, even without these advantages, the level of organised use and sharing of information is much higher than in 'routine' CID work on divisions. As we shall see, the key action in securing evidence is the *raid*, in which several members of Squad – including supervisors – normally assist the officer who has researched a particular 'job'. This is preceded by a briefing, in which the latter lays out what is known and what to expect. Such meetings are much less common on division, where, unless they are dealing with an exceptionally complex or serious case, officers tend to undertake the whole investigative process, from intelligence-gathering to arrest, on their own or with one partner, often with the rest of their colleagues having only vague knowledge of the cases they are handling or the information they have received.

Informants

All the Drugs Squad officers we spoke to highlighted the centrality of informants to making drug cases. Two typical comments were:

> 'Drugs squads live on informants. Without informants you get nowhere.'

> 'Practically all our work comes from informants'.

Analysis of small samples of cases also confirmed this view. In one force, where we examined 26 current or recently completed drug investigations, it was clear that in at least 19 of the 26 an informant had been the primary information source.

Informants not only play a vital role in the initial identification of people who are dealing, but can provide continuous up-to-date information on the best time to 'strike' to catch them with drugs. Where a good informant is in place, this can considerably reduce the length of an investigation and almost guarantee a successful conclusion to the case. For instance, the Operational Order of one case read as follows:

> 'Information has come via an informant that the following persons are supplying cannabis resin. The informant has stated that 'A' supplies flattened and rolled cannabis (unwrapped) and keeps the gear on the window-sill in the lounge at . . . His supplier is believed to be 'B', who supplies one quarter to one half ounce deals to various street dealers.'

> 'After consultation with informant to establish if A or B are in possession of cannabis resin. This being so, to execute simultaneous search warrant at both houses.'

The result was five and a half ounces recovered in a block from A and ten ounces and £3,765 in cash recovered from B.

In this case, we can see how the quality of information from the informant was the central feature of how the case was made. The informant named and located the dealer; located the exact place where the drugs were stored; and established the most effective time to execute the warrant. In many cases, however, informants are not so well placed and may contribute little more than 'putting a name in the frame', which will then require intensive intelligence gathering through surveillance to determine when to strike.

A similar pattern is to be found in the RCS, where, again, the importance of informants cannot be overstressed. For instance, in one branch office, in at least 34 out of 50 recent operations the targets had originally been identified by informants. They also provide the up to date intelligence which enables surveillance to be directed to those times when the target is actively engaged in committing offences. Without informants, therefore, not only would knowledge about who was committing the more serious offences be scarce, but it would also entail a far greater use of surveillance – which would be prohibitively expensive in terms of time and money. As one branch coordinator explained:

> 'The most expensive way of policing is through surveillance, the cheapest way is through informants, and I have to try and achieve a balance in the office between the two.'

The cost and resource implications of surveillance – which ties up the whole syndicate, at a cost, one DI estimated, of £1,500 per day – mean that, while it can be productively used for initial intelligence gathering, to 'house' a target and to document his or her routines, associates and vehicles, it is generally not feasible to use it as a blanket measure continuing until the target happens to engage in criminal activity.

By the strategic use of informants who are close to the target, information about planned criminal enterprises or major drug buys, knowledge of when he or she will be in possession of stolen or illicit materials, can be gained far more effectively. For instance, in a case involving a team of travelling burglars, the DI explained that:

> 'One of the lads in the office had an informant who was living close to the target, and was deployed to keep a lookout for when particular vehicles were arriving at the location, which indicated that the team were about to operate'.

And in another, which had involved a series of Post Office robberies, an informant rang in to say that the team was about to set off in the next hour to commit another crime. A surveillance team was hastily assembled, the targets were followed for over 150 miles and were observed breaking into a retail outlet and stealing over £5,000 worth of goods.

Surveillance

As explained earlier, the basic unit of organisation of the RCS is the syndicate, comprising twelve DSs and DCs. The functional importance of the syndicate is that it provides the basic unit for surveillance. Whereas cases are handled by teams under the direction of the Detective Sergeants, mobile surveillance is carried out by the whole syndicate, playing a service role for one of its constituent teams. It is the ability of the syndicate to provide a dedicated surveillance capacity for its member teams that differentiates the RCS from other investigative units. The fact that the size of the basic unit of organization is determined by the capacity to undertake surveillance, highlights the importance of surveillance work to the RCS. Activity charts provided by one Branch indicated that surveillance work accounts for about 50 per cent of its total workload; expressed in terms of days worked per person, eleven of the standard 22 working days per month are spent undertaking surveillance.

The resource intensive nature of the work is necessitated by the practical difficulty of not losing the target while at the same time remaining covert. To be effective, and to avoid the possibility of detection, a minimum of five vehicles and, ideally, the addition of a motor cyclist, are needed. The RCS's advantage over virtually all other branches of the police service in terms of surveillance capacity is illustrated by several other features – all, again, cost-intensive. First, they have a dedicated fleet of vehicles which are regularly changed to avoid identification by targets. Second, they have a covert encrypted radio system which enables discreet surveillance that cannot be eavesdropped by readily available commercial equipment. Third, all new officers are trained in mobile surveillance techniques and taught standardised operating procedures. Finally, while Drugs Squads usually have ready access to some photographic equipment, the RCS can draw upon the extensive resources of each region's Technical Resource Units, which supplies branch offices with a panoply of specialist equipment ranging from high powered binoculars to video cameras, time lapse photography equipment, night vision equipment and a range of tracking, listening, and image enhancing devices.

Force Drugs Squads, while not having ready access to resources on this scale, also use surveillance techniques on a frequent basis. Some, however, are limited largely to static, rather than mobile surveillance. The true value of surveillance to Drugs Squads emerges where informants are not well enough placed to provide reliable information to indicate the best time and place to execute a raid. Surveillance allows officers to establish patterns of activity of the main target, and in particular, times when there are significant numbers of callers at premises used by the target, which may be indicative of purchases taking place and the presence of a large quantity of drugs.

Surveillance can also play an important role in providing evidence of drug dealing. Used in this way, its purpose is to produce a record of the movements of the accused and of his or her contacts with others. The main kinds of records used are observational logs, still photographs and video recordings.

In an ideal case, then, surveillance contributes three major elements which can be used in combination to build up evidence for the charges of 'supply' or 'possession with intent to supply':

i. The construction of a written and photographic record of the activities of the target and his or her dealings with others

ii. Indications of the best time to raid premises in order to recover physical evidence in the shape of a substantial quantity of drugs and any drug-related 'paraphernalia' (eg scales, cutting tools, packaging materials, records of customers and money owing, as well as counter surveillance equipment such as radio scanners).

iii. The identification of persons thought to have just purchased drugs from the target premises, who may be stopped and searched on leaving. If found in possession, such people may be persuaded (eg by indications that they will only be cautioned if they cooperate) to give information about, or evidence against, the dealer.

Two brief case examples will illustrate these three processes and, especially, their importance and mutual dependence in the more difficult task of proving 'supply'. In the first case, observations had been mounted on the premises over five days. For each of these an observation log was kept, which recorded details of everybody who called at the house. For example:

11.07   Male walks down bank and into target premises with small plastic bag in right hand.

11.36   Male white, beard, comes from target premises transfers small packet from left to right hand, runs to van and drives off.

11.54   Male white, fair hair clutching something in right hand, returned to car and drives away.

In addition to the log, a video recording was simultaneously made of the target premises, providing a photographic record of the activities detailed in the logs. Further, a number of the persons observed entering the target premises and leaving shortly afterwards were known by the officers mounting the surveillance. Following the advice of the Crown Prosecution Service, a list of names (where known) was included as part of the evidence, indicating any drug convictions.

In the second case, static observation had been mounted on four consecutive days. This formed the basis of the written log, and although there was no photographic corroboration, it provided the main evidence of 'supply'. In all, there were over 75 entries on the logs, detailing the activity of the two accused and the comings and goings of various people to the back door of the house. One entry, for example, read as follows:

'Curtain pulled back by target, door opened. Youth in dark coat entered, other two remained in yard. After five seconds 1st youth comes out of house he was then handed an object by 'A'. All three then walked into the outer yard 1st youth showed 2nd male a brown object in his right hand. All three left the yard.'

In themselves, the entries in these logs did not provide evidence of criminal activity: a 'brown object' may be chocolate not cannabis, and even with a video recording this evidence is only supportive rather than substantive. However, when drugs were found on the premises, the logs became crucial in sustaining a charge of 'supply' rather than simple 'possession'.

The process in non drug related investigations taken on by RCS is often similar to that described above, using a combination of background intelligence, surveillance and informants in order to create a picture of what is occurring and the evidential basis for subsequent charges. In some cases, the starting point is a 'whisper' from an informant, in others the identification of a pattern in known offences. In either event, the investigative and evidence-gathering process can be characterised as the establishment of a series of evidential links between events and people. For example, forensic evidence from, and the *modi operandi* used in, recorded cases of particular kinds of serious offence may be sifted and analysed, sometimes on a national scale, in order to establish links between them. The further step of linking specified offenders to such a series of offences may be achieved through informants, though it will usually require other forms of evidence to convict them. For example, a case involving the theft of cheques in a series of burglaries necessitated the forensic examination of several hundred stolen cheques and pattern analysis of where and when they had been presented. The forensic evidence was used to link the offenders to the encashment of the stolen cheques, while the pattern analysis demonstrated that this had occurred on numerous occasions within days of the particular burglary being committed and in the same part of the country. The group could therefore be charged with conspiracy to commit burglary, rather than simply cheque offences.

Linking a target to associates, again, may be achieved in a variety of ways, for example through surveillance, information from informants, or through the use of a facility which lists all numbers dialled from a nominated telephone. In one case, an informant took a photograph of the target team together, which was later used to provide evidence of association.

However, in most RCS cases, as in Drugs Squad cases, the ideal is to apprehend the target in the act of committing a serious offence. As noted earlier, information about when this may occur is achieved through the use of informants, or through surveillance to establish a pattern of events (eg a team 'casing' premises they are planning to burgle). A high proportion of the RCS target operations we analysed had culminated in surveillance based 'strikes'.

Supervisory Structures

Unlike Divisional CID work, in which cases have traditionally been dealt with in an individualistic, if not competitive, framework, the work of the RCS – and, to some extent, Drug Squads – can more appropriately be characterized as teamwork. This is reflected also in supervisory structures which, in some respects, are considerably tighter. This is particularly the case when a group of officers – or the whole office – are working on one particular 'job', for instance in putting together information, mounting surveillance or executing a raid. In such circumstances, everybody is briefed, each has a specific role and considerable control is exercised by those in charge.

However, the other side of working in these squads is the expectation that individual officers will 'independently generate information about active criminals. All Drugs Squads, and some Regional Crime Squads, also expect individuals to produce a satisfactory number of arrests on their own initiative, not assisted by the full team. (There was a considerable difference between the two RCSs we visited, in this respect: one put low priority on individual arrests, arguing that these could 'tie officers up in paperwork' when they were needed to work on the main 'packages'.) When working in this individualistic mode, officers were often subject to no more direct supervision than those working on division – although, as we shall see, there were specific supervisory mechanisms in the RCS, relating to *contacts with informants*, which are of considerable interest and importance.

Regional Crime Squads

In the case of the RCS, the issue of supervision can be considered first of all in relation to recent changes in the rank structure. Prior to these changes, front-line supervision in the RCS was the responsibility of Detective Sergeants who each had under them only one Detective Constable. This one-to-one ratio was felt to be justified by the high level of autonomy that RCS officers were granted (except, as noted, when taking part in coordinated operations), the seriousness of the offences that they were dealing with, and, above all, the reliance on criminal informants as the dominant source of current intelligence. However, owing to the full operational immersion of the Detective Sergeant, and the close working relationships that were consequently established between DSs and DCs, Sergeants came to be seen – and acted – as little more than senior constables. The primary difference between a DC and a DS was that sergeants were expected, through the use of their wider criminal and police contacts, to generate more intelligence to help maintain the flow of 'jobs' into the office. Although they had a formal supervisory role, it was mainly limited to the routine signing of pocket books, expense claims and overtime sheets.

In an effort to increase the supervisory content of the Sergeant's role, a 1987 Home Office Directive instructed that:

> 'In order to make Sergeants' responsibilities for supervision more effective, there should be a common ratio of one Sergeant to three Constables'. [HOC 28 1987]

The major rationale for such a shift was that, rather than facilitating close supervision, the one-to-one ratio actually reduced its effectiveness by undermining the necessary distance between supervisor and supervised. Although the changes proposed by the circular have now been fully implemented, there is little evidence that it has produced any major change in supervisory practice. As one RCS Detective Inspector explained:

> 'Even though a DS is supposed to be a supervisor, he gets tied up with his own work. Often the DCs will be working completely on their own. But the DCs are self-disciplined so they just get on with the work ... We have a briefing once a week and then you say get on with it.'

Another DI said, similarly:

> 'The DS's are doing what they've always done, they are still fully operational and see themselves as part of the team'.

This middle management view was also supported by most DCs and DSs we spoke to, both groups stressing that there was little differentiation between their roles in practice. A few examples of their comments are given below:

> 'The Sergeant and I are the same age, same service and have the same outlook, there is no difference in rank here, he would never impose it on me, it wouldn't be appropriate. Everyone has to muck in – you're all part of a team'.

> 'Supervision in the RCS isn't like uniform. I don't go to Barry and ask his permission to do something, I don't call him Sergeant and he doesn't expect it. We put everything together as a team.'

> 'In terms of supervision, the way I do it is to lead, by example, from the front. But it is difficult, you've got your own work to do and then you're still supposed to keep an eye on everybody else ... The key element is that you have got to know what is happening. Obviously when you are out working with someone you know what

they are doing but that means two officers are working on their own, so it's got to be about trust.'

In reality, then, the formal change in supervisory ratios has had little effect on the DS-DC relationship. This is hardly surprising. In practical terms, Sergeants are still seen, and see themselves, as investigators. Moreover, they do not believe that much supervision is necessary, owing to the high calibre of DCs on the squad. As one Sergeant explained:

> 'DCs require far less supervision than Uniform Officers because so many PC's are in a rut and there are so many new ones. To get into the CID you have to prove that you are a worker by bringing in the bodies. In the RCS they are even more highly motivated, not only do they want to be detectives but they really want to do the job.'

Drugs Squads

In the Drugs Squads, a not dissimilar picture emerged. Again, the Sergeant's role was defined as investigative rather than supervisory. Two comments from DSs were:

> 'I'm even more operational here than I was on division. I put in as much work as any of the lads in the office and carry the same, if not a higher caseload. If I wasn't operational then there would be one of the team without a partner and I honestly don't think I'd have enough to do.'

> 'There's not a great deal of difference between a DC and a DS. I still put up jobs, I tend to see myself more as a senior constable.'

The second of these DSs went on to say that he had been given the job of reorganizing the drugs cupboard. This mammoth task had meant that 'for six months all I did was live in the cupboard' and as a consequence his team had been largely left to its own devices.

Many other comments we heard echoed those made on division, about the dependence on trust rather than supervision, about the impossibility of keeping tabs on everything DCs do, about the lack of clear role distinctions, and about the lack of necessity for supervision because of the high motivation of officers (the latter being seen as even greater on squads). A few examples will suffice to give the flavour:

> 'People who are in here deserve to be here, they have proved themselves and to be quite honest they don't need to be supervised because they want to work and they want to catch criminals.'

> 'You can't be looking over their shoulders all the time, you've got to give them the credence that they deserve and the leeway to do a good job.'

> 'If people want to bend the rules you can't stop them, you can't be everywhere at once.'

'Here I expect a sergeant to be a workmate, all of us in the office come to work so we don't need supervising, we're not out screwing or on the drink, and the DS knows that.'

'You're working very much on your own initiative and if the guv'nors decided to come down hard then there would be no-one left in here, or there'd be no results, they've got to give you room to manoeuvre.'

Comments

The central ethos of selection for CID work and, above all, for force squads and the RCS, is that detectives are highly motivated, and are capable of generating and carrying out their own work with minimal supervision. Given that the dominant view of supervision was that it was to ensure that officers were working hard, it is hardly surprising that 'general' supervision (as opposed to specific procedural, or 'bureaucratic' forms of supervision – see below) was seen as a marginal topic in these higher levels of CID work. Again, as on division, officers did not see supervisory mechanisms as relevant for ensuring compliance with legal or procedural rules which might lead to a miscarriage of justice: when we asked interviewees what mechanisms were in place to prevent such problems, no one mentioned the role of the Detective Sergeant. Rather, it was felt that the safeguards built into PACE were sufficient.

However, the absence of a strict supervisory content to the Detective Sergeant's role should not be taken to imply that there are not other controls in place to prevent 'rule bending' or malpractice. It is merely to point out that *'supervision' is not generally seen as the way to achieve this.* In the next section, we look at some other control mechanisms in relation to what we see as the most important 'weak spots' arising from the nature of proactive investigations by squads.

Potential 'weak spots and mechanisms of control.

Introduction: differences from reactive work

In this section, as in the previous two chapters, we set out to identify potential 'weak spots' – areas in which the dangers of error or malpractice appear to be strongest – in the particular investigative context we are examining. We shall discuss these within the framework of what we have already identified as two of the most important elements of the investigative armoury used by proactive squads: surveillance and the use of informants.

Before doing so, it is important to emphasise two fundamental differences between CID work on division and that in the RCS and Drugs Squads, which have a bearing on the relative risks of malpractice. First, we have noted that in divisional CID work, which concentrates on past cases, there is often only weak physical or eye-witness evidence to link an offender to the offence – a factor which places heavy reliance upon confession as a tool for securing a conviction and creates some temptation or pressure to 'bend the rules' or 'gild the lily' in acquiring this or other forms of verbal evidence. In the RCS and Drugs Squads, by contrast, because the work is largely self initiated and focussed upon future offences, interview evidence is in many cases not vital to conviction. With adequate time to plan and the main strategy being to time a 'strike' for a moment when the 'target' is in possession of incriminating evidence or in the act of committing an offence, *most of the necessary evidence is gathered before, or at the time of, arrest*. Consequently, officers have far less reason to consider fabricating verbal evidence or coercing admissions.

Secondly, squads are not normally judged in terms of clear up rates, which make no sense in relation to proactive work. As both RCS and Drugs Squad officers explained, although there was some pressure to produce 'results', this was of a different kind to the pressure to maintain the detection rate. Numbers of arrests were regarded as important in some squads, but there was no sense of the 'sausage factory' atmosphere of divisional CID work. Much more attention was paid to the *quality* of arrests. Where Drug Squads were concerned, there was little incentive to 'bend rules' to convict minor offenders: if they wished to catch large numbers of drug users for possession, there were so many, so visible, that officers would have no need to fabricate evidence. Rather, they earned recognition and status from the bigger cases, involving substantial dealers. According to one DS:

> 'The office can live in the glory of one good bust for a very long time'.

Regional Crime Squads, too, have the 'luxury' of pursuing particular offenders for lengthy periods (sometimes, over a year) without intense pressure for a 'result'. Here, despite the high costs of the operations[4] and the seriousness of the offences concerned – two features which RCS cases have in common with HOLMES investigations, and which, in the latter case, can be the source of substantial pressures on the SIO to solve a case in quick time – the lack of public knowledge or emotion about most cases allows the RCS team to work at a leisurely pace without any interest from the media. Any pressure for 'results', therefore, tends to be more general and more periodic – perhaps when it becomes apparent that a team has produced very little over the past year. But even then, the independence of the RCS from the main internal source of such pressure, senior management at force headquarters, leaves them with the

---

[4] Operations were regularly costed. The sample we looked at in one RCS ranged from a few hundred to several thousand pounds, with a median cost around £800.

less difficult task of justifying their performance to the various inter-force committees to which they report.

Bearing these comments in mind, let us now look at potential 'weak spots', and precautionary measures taken, in the specific areas of surveillance and the use of informants.

Surveillance

As stated earlier, the main results of surveillance activities are crime intelligence and indications of the best time to 'strike', products which, in themselves, are unlikely to affect the correctness of convictions. Indeed, as an intelligence gathering strategy, the use of surveillance – and breaches of rules governing its use – probably raises more questions about civil liberties than about miscarriages of justice. Writers such as Gary Marx (1989) have expressed considerable concern about a rapid growth, in the USA particularly, in the use of sophisticated technological devices for observing people and listening to their private conversations, without a corresponding development of effective guidelines and controls on their use. Unfortunately, although acknowledging its importance, we were unable in the time available to follow up this issue in any depth in relation to the RCS and are not in a position to judge whether, or to what extent, there may be a cause for concern here. In theory at least, there are fairly strict internal controls in existence in this country. The use of telephone 'taps', concealed microphones, tracking devices and printed meter checks, for example, is subject to high level authorization. Requests have to be made to the branch commander, who will then forward the request to the Chief Constable. The guidelines state that the requesting officer and authorising officers must be satisfied that the offence warrants such serious measures, that normal methods have been tried and failed and that the use is likely to result in an arrest. However, although some information was available about the number of such requests granted (for example, in one of the regions under study, just under 100 requests had been granted during a period of twelve months), there were no figures on the number of requests denied.[5]

When used as *evidence*, rather than merely for information gathering, surveillance contains other potential dangers. For example, where observation logs provide the sole form of evidence about meetings between drug dealers and customers, unsubstantiated by photographic

---

[5] Officers claimed that the procedure was by no means a 'rubber stamping exercise'. For example, a Branch Commander spoke of refusing to forward requests for authorisation if he felt they were unlikely to succeed, and one of the Inspectors complained bitterly of having his request for a phone tap, which also requires the authorisation of the Home Secretary, 'knocked back' at force level. However, such anecdotal evidence tells us little about the effectiveness of the controls.

evidence, there is the possibility of falsification either by strengthening what was claimed to have been seen or even by complete fabrication. Certainly, where static surveillance – which is usually carried out by only two officers – is concerned, the only guarantee of the integrity of the logs may be the integrity of the officers involved. However, with mobile surveillance, which is a team effort, proper pre-surveillance briefing (with a detailed written operational order outlining the nature and objectives of the surveillance) and post-surveillance debriefing (where the logs are verified by the whole team) do provide some protection against falsification. This is not only because any fabrication would have to involve a significant part of the team, but because properly conducted briefings create the *ethos* of a planned, rational, managed system, which is open to some scrutiny and supervisory control. While in the RCS such a system was the norm, this was not the case in other proactive units that we observed, there sometimes being no systematic debriefing, and no group verification of the logs.

Informants

i. Introduction

The other major strategy of RCS and Drugs Squad investigations involves the use of informants. With the current ACPO encouragement of more effective intelligence systems, their use is likely to become more widespread, not only in proactive squads, but also at divisional and subdivisional level. One of the factors behind this trend is a perceived need within the police to counteract the limitations placed by PACE on traditional, confession-based investigative strategies, by seeking to strengthen other sources of evidence and information.

CID officers described a range of motives for people becoming informants, ranging from simple financial self-interest to revenge and to fear of arrest. While several senior officers we spoke to claimed that financial gain was often the prime incentive for people to inform, DCs tended to regard it as less central to their motives – not least, because the size of the payments that could be made were generally small considering the risks the informants ran. In the force Drugs Squads, for example, £200 was considered an exceptional payout and although larger sums were quite frequently paid by the RCS, these were still generally in the hundreds rather than the thousands of pounds.[6]

While money may be a motive for informants not in immediate danger of arrest or imprisonment themselves, a large number of people –

---

[6] It should be noted that, in Divisional CID work, typical fees paid were extremely low – typically in the area of £5.

perhaps the majority – who inform do so when they face (or think they face) conviction and hope, by so doing, to 'limit the damage' or to avoid it entirely. At the extreme are the so-called 'supergrasses', most of whom face many years in prison, but are prepared to give a great deal of information in return for the chance of a greatly reduced sentence.[7]

The latter, however, are rare, even in the context of RCS work. The more mundane reality is the striking of informal 'deals' of various kinds, often vague and without guaranteed delivery on the part of the police. Interestingly, officers in the Drugs Squads were more open with us on these matters than divisional CID officers (or, indeed, the RCS), seeing such strategies as a legitimate form of pressure on suspects – in fact, a vital weapon in their work. As has been emphasised, the currency of *information* is central to their operations, and they are less interested in making 'deals' in order to obtain confessions (as in 'routine' CID work) than in order to obtain information about drug dealers. First of all, they often do not *need* confessions from those caught in possession of drugs – as noted, this is usually sufficient evidence in itself. And secondly, they are more prepared to 'go easy' on minor drug offenders, who are not difficult to arrest again at any time, in order to 'catch bigger fish'. A number of specific forms of 'preferential treatment' sought by arrested persons were mentioned:

- the granting of bail

- reductions in charges (eg from 'supply' to 'possession')

- the dropping of charges against associates (eg spouses)

- lower sentences ('a word to the judge')

- informal immunity from prosecution

A few comments from DCs and DSs on these subjects are listed below:

'I always like to try and get a conspiracy charge on the sheet. For some reason they don't like that, you can always drop it but it means that you've got something to bargain with'.

'Where you've got a husband and wife locked up and jointly charged, you can put it to him that we could get the wife off, if he is prepared to cooperate'.

---

[7] In the late 'seventies and early 'eighties, it was quite common for major informants to be granted immunity from prosecution by the DPP, but this was discontinued after serious disquiet about the whole 'supergrass' system. Nowadays the main incentive offered is an official request to the judge to consider a discount on sentence as a reward for cooperation.

'If I'm looking for an informant, I'm looking for someone who is weak. Heroin addicts are the easiest, you can lock them up, and lock them up again until they agree'.

Two points to note are (i) that some of the 'offers' involve consequences that would probably not have followed anyway, even if the 'deal' were refused (for example, attempts to press higher charges might have little chance of success), so to some extent the police are relying on the fear and ignorance of the accused in believing that the options are real; and (ii) that delivery of 'promises' is dependent upon the cooperation of people outside the police. For example, requests that judges or the parole board take into account the fact that an offender has helped the police by giving information about accomplices can be formally conveyed to these bodies (in the case of judges, via the CPS), but what weight they give to this fact is a matter for them.

ii. Problematic issues

The process of recruiting and using informants, then, can be seen as an exchange relationship, where the police are able to hold out the promise of favourable treatment or financial reward in exchange for intelligence. This exchange relationship is based on the discretionary powers that officers have in deciding whether to arrest and charge, whether to object to bail and whether to charge accomplices, as well as their ability to make recommendations of leniency to the court and to offer payment.

Many of these strategies, which rely on individual detective entrepreneurship, are of extremely low visibility, and subject to minimal supervisory control. Where informants are used only for intelligence gathering purposes, these factors may raise questions about police conduct, civil liberties, and the effectiveness of internal rules to regulate officer behaviour, but they are unlikely to result in miscarriages of justice, because in most cases the evidence to prosecute will be gained independently of the informant. On occasion, however, informants are used in open court as evidence givers. For instance, in a case we examined which involved the importation of drugs, one of the main couriers was persuaded to turn Queen's evidence in return for limited immunity from prosecution, agreed by the CPS. His evidence formed the core of the prosecution case to prove conspiracy to import drugs against a number of people. In such cases there are, of course, clear dangers that the informant, out of his or her own self interest, may exaggerate the involvement of others, and fabricate some of the evidence in an effort to strengthen the prosecution case. In this particular case, the defence alleged that he had been afforded financial and other rewards as well as being allowed inter-prison visits from his wife, seeking thereby to show that his evidence was based upon inducement.

This issue can be further clouded in the case of 'participating informants'.[8] For instance, in another case, an informant was used to make a purchase from a drugs dealer. Immediately afterwards, the premises were raided and the informant arrested along with the dealer. The informer then made a statement giving evidence of his purchase. In this case, the dealer pleaded guilty in the face of incontrovertible evidence. However, the role of the informant was never disclosed to the court, nor to the accused, his solicitor, or to the CPS, which means that a possible line of defence, that of incitement, was denied to the accused.

Again, an officer described how he had recently completed a major case involving 'supply' charges. An informant had been involved in the transportation of the consignment. As he explained:

> 'You don't reveal to the court that they were participating, and it's not as though they are going to know. It's so much red tape, you've got to get the ACC's authority and fill in all the paper work, so you bend the rules and don't tell them'.

It is these low visibility practices, we suggest, whose disclosure rests solely in the hands of the police, which are the most vulnerable to procedural rule bending and could potentially give rise to unsafe convictions. This danger is increased by the paucity of training throughout the CID (with the exception of the RCS – see below) in the handling and supervision of informants and, in many forces, the limited written guidelines and instructions. Apart from those in the RCS, none of the detectives to whom we spoke had received anything other than a cursory lecture on informants. The main effect of this is that officers learn to handle them only by watching and listening to more experienced colleagues. There is, of course, a danger that this learning process leads them into undesirable informal working rules and practices. Two comments from officers in a force squad sum up the problem:

> 'I think we were given all the guidelines in training, but that was eleven years ago and you soon forget them. I suppose I learnt through talking to John and seeing how he did it.'

> 'I have received absolutely no instruction in the running of informants. I had to learn it myself. We need to be taught how to use informants, because it is very difficult to maintain a professional relationship, you are treading a fine line, sometimes they want

---

[8] Although there is a body of case law, together with force guidelines limiting their use and requiring the permission of the Regional Coordinator or Assistant Chief Constable, this is still a grey area, lacking clear definitions of 'participation'.

something that you can give them, and sometimes you can't, but you need clear ground rules to make the decision.'

iii. Mechanisms of control

In the RCS, there are more explicit guidelines and procedures relating to informants than are found either at force or divisional level. Although they have little to say about the recruitment of informants, they do provide a system specifically designed to regulate dealings with them, especially in the area of payments. These are set out in a nine page memorandum, which is considerably more detailed than that found elsewhere. The memorandum covers the system of registration, management, day to day contact, and financial dealings with informants. It stands in stark contrast to most other areas of the CID, where procedures are much more haphazard.

The central principles governing the system are that informants, as it were, 'belong' to the police service rather than to the 'handler', and that proper supervision is imperative to ensure procedural propriety and to protect officers from false accusation. To effect this, all informants, whether paid or unpaid, should be *registered*. The registration process is designed to ensure the anonymity of the informant and will be the only document which lists his or her true identity, all others using a pseudonym. Once registered, the informant will be assigned a *handler*, normally the detective who recruited him or her, and a *controller*, who will generally be the Branch Commander.

The controller is responsible for ensuring that all contacts between the informant and the handler (which should, as far as possible, be notified in advance) are carried out in accordance with official guidelines, that all contacts are properly logged, and that a full intelligence report is prepared on the content of each meeting. He or she also evaluates the quality of the intelligence gained, in terms of its source and content.

In many forces, simplified versions of this registration system have been introduced in headquarters squads and, increasingly, in divisional CID offices. Nevertheless, in these contexts, the successful operation of such systems is often handicapped by the reluctance of detectives to register all informants and to fill in contact sheets. This derives partly from practical problems: as one DC in a force squad stated, it was not possible to log every contact, because informants were 'always ringing up, and always wanting to see you, and the governor would go mad if you went to him with every contact'. It also relates to a long tradition within the CID of 'keeping information to oneself', born of rivalry and competitiveness. Information is 'safer in your head' than on official contact sheets and intelligence forms, which enable other officers to use 'your' intelligence.

This tradition appeared to have been overcome to a considerable extent in the RCS, where the concepts of teamwork and sharing of information are strongly emphasised by managers, and where officers are rewarded as much for producing good intelligence as for making their own arrests (though even here, we were told, there is a tendency to develop information for some time before disclosing it to the group). Outside the RCS, however, Sergeants generally conceded that it was extremely difficult, if not impossible, to ensure that all contacts were regulated, although this did not concern them unduly. A typical comment from a Drugs Squad DS was:

> 'You've got to rely on their discretion, and of them coming to see you and letting you know what's going on. I think most of the lads comply'.

It has to be remembered, of course, that the detective-informant relationship is built upon the gradual development of trust. It is a highly personalised and private business, which, on a day-to-day basis, may not be conducive to 'hands-on' supervision. As one Sergeant explained:

> 'You have to supervise from one pace back. You know who they're going to meet and when they are meeting and then you want to know what took place.'

The effect of this is that supervisors – and, indeed, controllers in the RCS – are almost completely dependent upon the officer reports as a basis for assessing, evaluating and regulating contacts. As one DI Controller stated,

> 'I have to make the decision as to whether the officer is running the informant or is the informant running the officer. That is not easy, because it will depend on what the officer tells you. He can embellish it, so in the end you've got to judge.'

Throughout the CID, the most highly regulated aspect of all informant dealings is that of monetary payments. The RCS is exceptionally strict in this respect, owing to a clear recognition that, in dealing with criminal activity involving thousands (and sometimes millions) of pounds and in paying some informants considerable sums, if there is one area in which there is a real danger of 'the wheel coming off', it is that of corruption or misappropriation of cash. In the RCS, even claims for under ten pounds are dealt with by the Branch Commander, while any claim in excess of this amount involves the completion, in triplicate, of a request form, endorsed by the Branch Commander and forwarded to the Regional Coordinator for approval. All monies subsequently paid out are supervised by an officer of at least the rank of DI, who must witness the handing over of the money, and get a signed receipt for it, even if the name used is fictitious.

Again, however, although rules in force throughout the CID prohibit officers from giving money to their informants unless officially sanctioned, these are in practice very difficult to enforce, even in the RCS. It is not unheard of, we were told, for officers to use their own money or their meal allowance money to 'oil the works' with small cash payments, thus avoiding the official structures:

> 'We spend a lot of money on informants, we have to. If your informants are skint you've got to give them something, and you don't get it all authorised, but you can get some of it back through your meal allowance.'

Nevertheless, although it is impossible to supervise the day to day interaction between detectives and informants, it should be said that the RCS system does provide a clear and explicit set of guidelines for registration, intelligence evaluation and the regulation of financial dealings with informants. Importantly, it recognises the inherent dangers in such relationships and attempts to provide a realistic system of supervision and control, which goes some way to minimising the chances of impropriety. It is encouraging to see that many of its elements have been incorporated into a new set of national guidelines on the management of informants, drawn up by a working group of the ACPO Crime Committee (ACPO 1992). If adopted by all forces, in all CID contexts, these guidelines would encourage a far more coherent set of practices than are now evident.

Management information

We conclude this chapter with brief comments about another important difference we noted between the RCS and other specialist units that we visited. This was the existence of a comprehensive management information system, based upon a set of monthly returns by each branch office to the Regional Co-ordinator. The returns cover the full range of managerial information, and consist of two basic types of data: standard indicators relating to activity patterns, and indicators relating to personnel and establishment. In the former case, these indicators are based on information concerning the origin of target packages, the number and type of operations, the number of arrests, the number of intelligence reports submitted and the number of payments to informants. In the latter, they document, among other things, squad strength, deployments, holidays, overtime worked, days off for sickness, the specialist skills of each officer, length of service on squad, accidents involving police vehicles, and complaints against officers.

Whilst such a system may seem only marginally related to ensuring the integrity of squad work in individual cases, we would argue that it is of central importance. Firstly, as the report into the West Midlands Crime

Squad indicated, many of its problems could be related to the paucity of managerial control, leading to excessive overtime, prolonged secondments, and a blurring of terms of reference. In the RCS, the managerial information allows such issues to be monitored on a monthly basis, and because this information forms the basis of the Regional Coordinator's Bi-annual Report, information is systematically recorded and it is open to scrutiny from the Chief Constables Management Committee, HM Inspectorate of Constabulary, and the Executive Coordinator.

Secondly, and perhaps most importantly, the system promotes an *ethos* of strong managerial control and oversight, which is not merely symbolic. Certainly, our impression was of a system with clear lines of managerial responsibility, where the branch management team, consisting of the Inspectors and Chief Inspectors, saw their role as managerial rather than investigative.

8. Summary and Conclusions

We pointed out in Chapter Four that there is no general agreement on the extent of police malpractice in relation to investigations, nor can it be known how many people are wrongfully convicted, either through such malpractice or through genuine errors arising from weaknesses in the information or evidence generated in inquiries.[1] This basic absence of knowledge can lead the debate about 'miscarriages of justice' into somewhat fruitless arguments in which people align themselves, or are pigeon-holed by others, into two opposing camps: on the one side, the police and the 'pro-police', who argue that both miscarriages and malpractice have always been rare, that those that have occurred have been caused either by understandable human error or by occasional individual 'bad apples' and that, anyway, serious investigative malpractice has now been virtually eradicated by PACE and by internal reforms; and on the other side, the 'anti-police', who see wrongful convictions as common and malpractice as widespread, endemic and highly resistant to efforts to control it (most of which, they argue, have been half-hearted and toothless).

In this study, in which we did not set out to – nor could we realistically hope to – come to any conclusion about the extent of police malpractice, we have tried both to by-pass this question and to avoid the trap of associating ourselves with either broad 'camp'. Our starting point has been the undeniable fact that major miscarriages of justice – some of them caused by incompetent investigations (and/or, it is important to add, incompetence by judges, lawyers and juries), some by genuine error, but a disturbing number by proven police malpractice – as well as instances of systematic corruption, have come to light, not just in recent years, but, despite every effort to prevent them, periodically throughout the history of the CID. From this, we argue, it seems wise to assume that, however honest the majority of detectives may be, the potential exists for future events of a similar or related kind. Our focus, therefore, has been upon identifying where, precisely, the greatest risks of investigative error or

---

[1] NACRO recently made such an estimate, running into several hundreds of prisoners, and similar exercises have been attempted in the USA, also producing high estimates. However, such estimates cannot claim any reliability.

malpractice lie and what can best be done, through supervisory or other control mechanisms, to reduce them.

In pursuing this aim, we have looked (inevitably briefly) both at general features of the CID – its history, 'culture' and traditions, the selection, training and 'socialisation' of its officers, and its organisational structures – and at specific features of its three main styles of investigation. In each of the latter – 'routine' divisional CID work, major reactive investigations, and proactive investigations by specialised force and regional squads – we have tried, through observation, file analysis, interviews with interested parties and, above all, through lengthy discussions with CID officers of all ranks, to identify any potential 'weak spots' particularly relevant to that style of work. The weak spots may relate to particular ways in which evidence and information are gathered, to the organisation or supervisory structure of the detective unit in question, and/or to special features or problems its officers face. At the same time, we have emphasised that, while these 'weak spots' vary in significance according to the type of investigation (and, indeed, the type of crime under investigation) nearly all are, ultimately, related to underlying problems inherent in the culture and traditions of the CID and in the nature of detective work itself, as historically understood.

We begin this concluding chapter with a straightforward summary of Chapters Three to Seven, in which we presented our account of the fundamental issues and of particular problems associated with each of the three main types of detective investigation. We shall then set out what appear to us to be the most promising strategies for controlling the quality and integrity of investigations in general.

Summary of arguments and research findings

In Chapter Three, we introduced the concepts of 'reactive' ('offence based') and 'proactive' (offender based') styles of investigation. We pointed out that, although the first of these accounts for the bulk of investigative work and although the main indicator of investigative effectiveness (the clear-up rate) is predicated on the model of the police attempting to 'solve' each individual crime reported by members of the public, many arrests and detections derive from different circumstances. For example, detained suspects and prisoners admit to offences previously unknown to the police, police officers catch offenders 'in the act' and some investigations are based upon targeting known offenders or the identification of crime patterns, rather than responding to individual offences. We also noted that successful investigations much less often involve deducing 'whodunnit' in the classic Sherlock Holmes fashion, than producing sufficient evidence to charge an offender named or identified by the person reporting the offence.

We pointed out, further, that the majority of arrests and charges are produced by uniform PCs without assistance from the CID. Admittedly, most such cases result in non-custodial or only short custodial sentences and hence, if a wrongful conviction ensues, the cost to the accused is likely to be considerably less than that suffered in the case of a major crime. But this is no reason to ignore them as a possible source of mistakes, misdeeds and miscarriages. Indeed, we speculated that the safeguards provided by PACE may be less effective in these 'minor' cases, where the volume of throughput, combined with the other pressing duties on PCs, leaves little time for thorough checking of evidence, and where solicitors are less often present at interviews than in major cases. Unfortunately, as we were severely limited by time, and the study had to be restricted to CID investigations of more serious offences, we could do no more than note this possibility.

We drew attention in Chapter Four to the fact that the history of the CID has been bedevilled by periodic scandals, mainly involving corruption, fabrication of evidence and the mistreatment of suspects to obtain confessions. These types of malpractice, we suggested, are related to two fundamental problems inherent in what have become the two main CID functions (i.e., the gathering of intelligence about, and of sufficient evidence to convict, groups of 'known criminals'): the fact that, in order to obtain information about the activities of so-called 'villains', detectives have to have some informal contact with them in social settings; and the fact that obtaining sufficient evidence to convict them in court can be extremely difficult if strict attention is paid to their rights and to the official 'rules of the game'.

We noted that views about the magnitude of these problems, about how the police respond to them, about the kinds of control which should be exercised over that response, and about the effects of such controls on both police behaviour and the effectiveness of detective work, vary widely: we identified six different broad approaches, which we dubbed for convenience the 'bad apple', 'internal regulation', 'crime control' (or 'state necessity'), 'justice' (or 'due process'), 'reformist' and 'radical reformist' views. This combination of unknowns and contrasting views, together with the variety of investigative styles, makes the subject of the management and supervision of investigations a vastly complicated one. In the time available, we could do no more than map out its contours and comment on its problems in a variety of contexts. The areas we chose to examine most closely were 'routine' divisional CID work, major 'reactive' investigations using the HOLMES system, and the 'proactive' work of Drugs Squads and Regional Crime Squads.

Before doing so, however, we took a preliminary look at three other factors which impinge upon the behaviour and approach of CID officers in all these contexts. The first, the 'detective culture', comprises a broad set of attitudes and working practices which have grown up over many years and which many observers and, increasingly, senior police officers see as a major obstacle to change. It is related to a broader 'occupational culture' of the police as a whole, whose essential features, as identified in several academic studies, are 'solidarity' and 'secrecy', a tendency among the lower ranks to operate according to their own informal rules (many of which breach formal codes of practice, which they regard as unrealistic) and to protect each other from a potentially harsh disciplinary code by effectively disguising this behaviour from supervisory officers. The detective culture, it has been argued, is somewhat different, being characterised by a more individualistic and competitive approach and greater confidence that CID officers can 'sail close to the wind'. The latter confidence derives from the greater freedom of action they are granted, their superior grasp of legal niceties, and the different kind of relationship they tend to develop with front line supervisors. Other traditional features of this 'culture' are a self-image as part of an 'elite' group within the police service and – a feature which may be changing more rapidly than most – a 'macho' lifestyle characterised by long hours in male company, in which drinking in pubs has played a prominent part.

The perpetuation of this culture and its associated problems, we argued, has been assisted by a long term failure of CID training courses to address the realities and pressures of the job. Although training policy, like many of the other areas we discuss, is currently under review, the content of basic CID courses is still dominated by the teaching of criminal law and the rules of evidence; until very recently, little attention has been paid to ethical problems in crime investigation or, in particular, to the dangers of wrongful conviction.[2] Similarly, advanced CID courses have paid little attention to the special skills of supervising detectives, leaving supervisory training for DIs and DSs to the general promotion courses which tend to concentrate on uniform officers' concerns. Moreover, we found that many CID officers do not attend courses until some time after their appointment, by which time they have undergone a process of 'apprenticeship' and 'socialisation' into the job, as it is understood and practiced by older colleagues: it is by then difficult for trainers to influence them to the same degree.

---

[2] See Morgan (1990), Irving and Dunnighan (1992).

The second factor discussed was that of the nature of supervisory relationships within the CID, in particular those between Detective Sergeants and Detective Constables. We noted the apparent paradox that, although supervisory ratios are much higher in the CID than in the uniform branch, it is widely agreed that there is 'less supervision' in the CID. We made three general points in this context, leaving more detailed discussion for later chapters. First, owing to the need for detectives to pursue inquiries in a flexible way over a wide area, they are often out of touch with the station and hence many of their day-to-day activities are invisible to supervisors. Second, because of this need, CID officers are selected in the first place partly on account of their perceived ability to work with 'a minimum of supervision'; sergeants' relationships with DCs, therefore, tend to be based largely on 'trusting them to get on with it', the DS providing, if anything, general 'leadership' rather than 'supervision'. We characterised this style of management, in Weberian terms, as 'charismatic' as opposed to 'bureaucratic' (or 'rational/legal'). Third, in line with this style, DSs have themselves remained 'close to the street', carrying their own caseloads and acting for much of the time simply as senior constables.

We pointed out that the effectiveness of this style of supervision in terms of preventing malpractice depends heavily upon the personal qualities of the supervisor and the overall integrity of the subordinates: essentially, it is as good as the people operating it. A 'good supervisor', while still inspiring his or her officers to produce results, will set a tone in which malpractice is regarded as deviant, and will look out for warning signs of such behaviour. On the other hand, a 'bad supervisor' may contribute to a slide in standards, either because he or she shows insufficient leadership or vigilance, or, worse, because he or she tacitly or openly condones rule-breaking. (The extreme consequences of bad supervision, we noted, have been seen in some of the major scandals, where higher ranking officers themselves became involved in systematic malpractice.) We therefore raised the question, left for later discussion, of whether a more formal and systematic approach is advisable.

The final problematic area we mentioned briefly in Chapter Four was that of the separate organisational structure of the CID, inasmuch as it has isolated detectives from the normal lines of management within each force. This has not only helped to sustain an unhealthy image of the former as a separate and 'elite' organisation (a 'firm within a firm'), but can cause particular problems at divisional level, where detectives are subject to a 'dual chain of command', being responsible both to the uniform commander and the CID hierarchy at headquarters.

We ended Chapter Four on a more positive note, acknowledging the existence of a considerable number of police initiatives aimed directly or indirectly at the problems we have raised and, indeed, of a general sense within the police that radical changes are necessary. We mentioned, in particular, the tone-setting pronouncements from ACPO, with their emphasis on 'quality of service'; ideas aimed at shifting investigations away from over-reliance upon confession evidence; efforts to change the role of Detective Sergeants; moves to incorporate the CID into the mainstream lines of management (including the possibility of removing the separate headquarters CID hierarchy); and developments in training and in selection practices.

In Chapter Five, we looked at the kind of work in which CID officers are most frequently engaged, that of processing the constant flow of crime reports at divisional level. Much of this work, we found, concerns offences of a relatively minor nature and is characterised by a series of essentially routine tasks, such as visiting scenes, taking statements, interviewing suspects, summarising tapes and collating evidence. It also entails working to time schedules, so officers are often to be seen in the office catching up on outstanding paperwork. At the same time, there is a strong element of unpredictability, in that the routine work is frequently interrupted by requests or instructions to help out colleagues with arrests, interviews, identity parades, or other contingencies, or, occasionally, to join a 'team' investigating a major crime.

We found that there is always in the background a set of 'pressures' on divisional CID officers, to 'perform'. This includes a general pressure on the office to maintain clear up rates at an acceptable level: if the monthly figures drop significantly, the DI can expect pointed questions from senior officers at headquarters and is likely to pass these on to DCs and DSs in the form of a 'pep talk' (or, as most put it, a 'bollocking'). It also includes a variety of pressures on individual officers to maintain a certain level of identifiable activity, particularly in the form of self-generated arrests and criminal intelligence. These individual pressures may be increased by a personal motivation to 'catch criminals', a desire for promotion (which is perceived – if to some extent wrongly – to depend largely upon performance as a 'thieftaker') or, ultimately, a wish to remain in the CID owing to the more interesting and rewarding career it is regarded as offering. The latter wish is strengthened by a common perception of the work of uniform PCs as increasingly dangerous, unpleasant and lacking in status, and by the view that to be 'returned to uniform' implies some kind of failure.

We then returned, in the context of divisional CID offices, to the question of supervision. When asked what they understood by this term, most officers (including DIs and DSs) expressed its main purposes as checking the quality of 'paperwork', providing morale-boosting leadership to the office, giving occasional advice on cases, allocating workloads equitably, ensuring that people are not 'skiving', and/or monitoring overtime and expenses claims. Very few mentioned, unprompted, the role of ensuring that rules protecting the rights of suspects are not 'bent' or broken and that officers act with integrity in investigations.

When we questioned them about this role, not only was it said to be difficult to perform owing to the nature of the work, but there was a strong feeling among supervisors that, generally speaking, one had to trust officers rather than 'go around looking over their shoulders'. Nevertheless, as most offices were small, DSs and DIs claimed to know all their staff personally and felt that they would soon 'get wind of' any persistent malpractice. There were also external channels of information about such matters, such as the complaints system and contacts with solicitors.

Despite these arguments, we raised a number of doubts about the appropriateness and effectiveness of this informal, trust based style of supervision. We drew attention again to negative factors in the environment of CID offices – especially the pressure for 'results' (on supervisors as well as DCs) – which could tempt officers towards malpractice. We noted the danger of supervisors, as a result of their own frequent 'hands on' involvement in investigations, failing to maintain sufficient distance from DCs and hence to exercise discipline when necessary. We also pointed out that, despite claims that CID offices are increasingly staffed by a 'new breed' of detectives who accept the spirit of PACE, there were still plenty of 'old hands' with traditional attitudes to be found. (It is worth adding that many of the middle management posts in the CID are filled by officers who learned their 'streetwise' detective skills before PACE.) Finally, we pointed out that, while it did appear that those 'brought up with PACE' were moving away from the 'macho' drinking culture of the past and were more receptive to changing ideas about how to investigate crime, their broad view of the investigative process remained closer to the 'crime control' than to the 'due process' model.

We next moved on to look at what we called potential 'weak spots' in the gathering of evidence, ie those techniques and types of evidence most likely to give rise to doubts or disputes. We concentrated in this chapter upon those most relevant to divisional CID work. We noted first of all that, although one of the most complex and controversial 'weak spots' is that of the conduct of interviews in police stations, this has been widely discussed elsewhere and, in order to make the best use of time, we had elected not to examine it in detail. The three areas we looked at specifically were i. conversations or 'interviews' which take place outside the formal setting of an interview room, ii. contacts with witnesses and statement taking and iii. police eye-witness accounts.

The first of these concerns the possibility that the PACE rules, while effectively regulating contacts between officers and suspects within police stations, have led detectives sometimes to 'rehearse' what will be said in taped interviews by means of informal communications with suspects, before (or even after) they come under the wing of the custody officer. It also raises questions about the reliability of records of such communications if they are subsequently put forward in evidence.

While acknowledging that the PACE rules discourage the conduct of 'interviews' in police cars or other informal settings, many detectives saw it as unrealistic to expect suspects to be conveyed to police stations in silence and stated that discussions relating to the alleged offence were quite common. Indeed, it was said, they were frequently initiated by the person arrested. The detectives we spoke to were often careful to distinguish between, on the one hand, 'deals' – agreements to seek more lenient treatment for arrested persons in return for admissions or information (a key proviso being that these are proposed by the suspect not the police) and, on the other, 'inducements' or 'threats'. The former were generally seen as justifiable within the rules and, indeed, as a valuable tool for successful investigations. The latter, by contrast, were clear breaches of PACE and/or the law and officers were distinctly more circumspect in discussing them. The general picture painted was one in which threats and, to a lesser extent, inducements, had come to be looked upon as 'deviant' activities, rather than, as in the past, fairly common practice. Consequently, officers who contemplated employing such methods could be less sure of colleagues' reactions and had to be careful to disguise them.

We commented, finally, that this is one of the areas in which nobody knows – and perhaps one can never know – the true extent of improper conduct. This, of course, presents a major problem for conscientious supervisors as well as for researchers.

The second potential 'weak spot' we identified concerned contact with witnesses, especially where the latter were known to be involved in other offences, or in criminal activity subsidiary to the case in hand. In such circumstances, there is a risk that the witness will make, or will be persuaded to make, untrue or exaggerated statements helpful to the police case, in the hope of receiving lenient treatment or avoiding charges altogether. We also looked briefly at the area of statement taking, where there is a danger of officers, who usually write the statement on the witness's behalf, prompting the latter to agree to subtly altered accounts of what they actually saw. As with threats and inducements to suspects, we noted, there is no way of knowing the extent of false evidence arising in these ways, but the risk is enhanced in divisional CID work by the lack of time to test the veracity of every witness statement, as well as by the obvious point that there is little incentive for officers (who, as we have noted, tend to favour the 'crime control' view of investigations) to undermine their own cases by following up discrepancies, if they are already convinced of the suspect's guilt.

The final potential 'weak spot' discussed in the context of routine CID work was that of eye witness evidence by officers. Examples were given of the temptation, in cases where they 'know' the suspect to be guilty but the evidence is weak, for officers to 'gild the lily' by claiming to have seen more than they actually did. Supervisors admitted that there was little they could do to prevent this occurring, beyond trying to engender an atmosphere in which such practices were regarded as deviant and 'out of order'.

In Chapter Six, we documented how, in contrast to the 'charismatic' style of supervision in Divisional CID investigations, major crime inquiries run from incident rooms – especially when employing the HOLMES system – are subject to a far higher degree of bureaucratic control and are based on teamwork rather than individual initiative. The scale of such inquires and their command over extensive resources means that all aspects of the case can be thoroughly investigated and corroborative evidence sought in all instances.

The bureaucratic control of such investigations is enhanced by a number of features. First, the comprehensive storage and retrieval capacity of the HOLMES system enables senior officers to review all documentation connected with the inquiry. Second, standardised administrative procedures govern the allocation, evaluation and cross-referencing of all materials. Third, there is a specialisation of functions within the team, with specific officers in designated roles responsible for specific tasks. Fourth, regular briefings and discussions are held and policy books are kept, producing a chronological record of (and the reasoning behind) the lines of inquiry followed, allowing periodic and retrospective reviews of the progress of the case. Finally, in the context of the supervision and management of such investigations, we noted that while the actions of individual officers working for outside inquiry teams were largely unsupervised, the product of their activity was subject to a number of thorough checks and controls, rendering individual malpractice both unlikely and extremely risky. (There is also little incentive for an individual DC, for example, to manipulate evidence, as his or her actions form only one minor input to the whole.)

In other words, in such inquiries any 'weak spots' which might generate malpractice and/or serious evidential errors, are of a different nature to those we have identified in 'routine' divisional CID work. Those that do exist, we suggest, tend to stem either from the nature of the case itself or from pressures on the senior investigating officer. The latter may include pressure from the media to catch a dangerous offender, as well as frequent internal reminders of the number of officers tied up in the inquiry and of the substantial financial costs which mount up every day. Almost by definition, too, HOLMES cases are among the most difficult to 'solve' and, despite the exceptional scientific resources available, good physical evidence is not always obtainable. In these circumstances, the SIO may be thrown back upon the familiar sources of witness statements and confessions. For example, we noted a recurring problem in a number of cases involving drug-related murders, where the main witnesses (most of them addicts) were either very reluctant to cooperate with the inquiry or else told blatant lies. The HOLMES system provides perhaps the best possible tool for cross-checking statements for consistency with others, but cannot provide a guarantee against misjudgements by the SIO about which line of inquiry to follow, about the appropriate credence to give to key statements, or about the acceptable level of pressure to put on reluctant witnesses to speak out.

In Chapter Seven, we shifted our attention to an examination of the contrasting investigative style of offender centred operations, typified by the work of the RCS and force Drugs Squads. In contrast to divisional work and HOLMES inquiries, we noted that such investigations are dominated by the use of surveillance and informants, enabling the targeting of offenders so that, ideally, they may caught 'red handed'. We argued that because of the longer time frame afforded to such inquiries and the strength of 'hard' evidence that they generated, the pressure to fabricate verbal evidence or to induce confessions by unacceptable methods was far less than in offender centred investigation.

As we had found in relation to other aspects of CID work, supervision was often focussed upon the product of investigations rather than the activity itself. Officers were often expected to work alone and in many respects unsupervised. And DSs, even more than on division, both saw themselves and acted as investigators rather than supervisors. On the other hand, a major advantage of the squad system is its 'team' approach and sharing of information when working on a large inquiry. In such cases, unless the whole unit is corrupted (the chances of which can be minimised by frequent movements in and out of the squad and, in the RCS, are greatly reduced by the presence of officers from different forces) the thoroughness and coordinated nature of the investigation makes it relatively unlikely that evidence will be doctored or fabricated.

The main potential 'weak spots' we identified were connected with the two central investigative tools used by proctive squads, surveillance and informants. We noted that there are civil liberties issues surrounding the use and control of telephone tapping and other listening devices, and that observation logs, particularly those compiled from static surveillance, are potentially open to fabrication (though these are not often used as key evidence in court). More importantly, relationships with informants contain inherent risks of corruption, as well as of excessive pressure being put upon some offenders to give evidence against others, with consequent doubts about its truth. There are particular dangers in the use of 'participating informants', which is increasing in frequency throughout the CID.

We found that, in the RCS, there was strong awareness of the risks of financial impropriety and that official payments to informants were tightly controlled. A clear system also existed to regulate and document the content of all meetings with informants, although this was not always followed in practice. Even so, we found it a good model to recommend to other CID units (including Drugs Squads), where controls tend to be considerably more lax.

In sum, we noted that intelligence led, informant based policing strategies were characterised by low visibility, making supervision inherently difficult. Nevertheless, we concluded that in the RCS, in particular, a combination of the strength of evidence gathered through surveillance, the separation of the Inspectors from day to day investigative responsibilities, clear and well documented procedures governing the use of informants and the selection of targets, a strong managerial ethos and a well developed management information system, made the risk of serious malpractice relatively low.

Possible ways forward

A programme for change

In the course of this report, we have identified a wide range of problems – general and specific, structural and 'cultural', ideological and practical – which stand in the way of efforts to ensure that criminal investigations are carried out in a a fair yet effective manner and that the chances of wrongful convictions or miscarriages of justice are minimised. In this concluding section, we shall put forward some tentative proposals for strategies to attack these problems. Many of these build upon ideas, initiatives and 'good practice' already being floated and implemented by progressive elements within the police service itself; others, more speculative, derive from our own reflections upon the situation as we perceived it. Some are of general application, while others – recognising the wide variety of investigative styles and organisational structures within the CID – are relevant to specific types of investigation or to specific elements within the investigative process.

We outline most of these proposals, in abbreviated form, under a series of broad headings, as follows:

    i. Taking the problem seriously
    ii. Attacking the 'culture'
   iii. Reducing pressures
   iv. Bridging the uniform-CID gap
    v. Clarifying responsibilities and separating functions
   vi. Seeking new investigative methods
  vii. Promoting openness

Finally, we offer a more extended exposition of our own idea of a new approach to meeting the problem of the 'invisibility' of much CID activity and the consequent difficulties of front-line supervision. This consists of a more formal system of monitoring, based on the notion of 'quality control'.

i. Taking the problem seriously

A *sine qua non* for effective reform of investigative practice is a genuine recognition within the police service that there is a problem. Several officers we spoke to – both uniform and CID – explained the recent damage to the reputation of the police largely in terms of a general failure of the CID to 'move with the times', in particular slowness to recognise and accept that PACE necessitated more than simply 'lip service': it demanded a real change in thinking and practice. There are signs now that this message is beginning to be heeded, particularly at very senior levels (as evidenced in the Strategic Policy Document and other general statements by ACPO) and, indeed, at the most junior level (the notion of the 'new breed' of DC), although some of our interviewees felt that middle management (particularly at Detective Inspector level) still contained a fair proportion of 'old school' detectives who were reluctant to accept that there was any need for change.

We found detectives generally willing to concede that unacceptable events have occurred in the past, although this concession was often qualified with 'neutralising' comments to the effect that some of those released on the grounds of unsafe convictions 'were probably guilty anyway', that 'the officers haven't been given the chance to tell their side of the story', or that such events were mainly restricted to particular forces or particular specialist squads and not part of a police-wide problem. There was also a widespread contention that 'such things couldn't happen now', owing to the advent of tape recording, in particular. In other words, if a true and lasting ideological shift is to occur, the depth and seriousness of the underlying problems need to be repeatedly reinforced. As one Chief Inspector put it:

> 'Words are not enough. As soon as the fuss dies down, things could easily revert to what they were ... The message has to be the old Churchillian line, "Lest we forget".'

To this end, a good starting-point might be a special educational programme, repeated at intervals, on miscarriages of justice and the part played in them by both sloppy investigative practices and 'rule-bending'. Thames Valley police, in implementing their 'Make Contact' programme – aimed at altering officers' manner in dealing with the public – required every officer in the force to attend special seminars on that subject. A similar strategy, together with strengthening the message in training and promotion courses, would demonstrate how seriously senior officers took the issue of integrity in investigations and might go some way towards altering 'hearts and minds'.

ii. Attacking the 'culture'

Part of such a programme would be aimed at raising CID officers' awareness of the faults in the traditional 'detective culture' ('macho' and 'elitist' attitudes, the belief that 'rules are there to be bent', excessive secrecy and suspicion of outsiders, and so on) and the ease with which young officers are sucked into it, almost without realising it. This, again, requires training, above all at an early stage, before the 'socialisation' process has had time to take effect. It also requires a serious look at selection processes. We would strongly support greater formalisation of these processes, giving more say both to senior uniform officers and to Personnel Departments. It was pointed out that the Singh case, which made it encumbent upon forces to introduce equal opportunity mechanisms into the selection process, has already had an important effect in this regard, with it now becoming common practice to advertise posts, to put the same questions to all candidates, and to take full notes of interviews. Reinforcement of such principles seems to us very important as a way of probing the attitudes and integrity of prospective CID officers and ensuring that they are not selected on their 'thieftaking' potential alone.

Similarly, it seems important to reinforce the trend towards limiting the amount of time that officers can spend in one posting or, indeed, in the CID without a break. HM Chief Inspector of Constabulary recently issued a document establishing the principle that officers should not normally spend more than three years in any particular squad (influenced, almost certainly, by the belief that the problems in the West Midlands Serious Crime Squad were partly due to fact that many officers had spent much longer periods in post). While there are disadvantages in that valuable experience may be 'wasted', these can be overcome by staggering appointments to achieve a good balance between experienced officers and neophytes. Indeed, the principle could be extended to the CID as a whole – say, a compulsory return to uniform duties for one year every three years, with a possibility of reappointment. (We have recently been told that one force may be considering a five-year limit to CID postings of any kind.) And, as is now policy – but not always standard practice – in many forces, we believe that promotion should always entail at least a short period in uniform.

iii. Reducing pressures

We have emphasised several times the 'pressure for results' which is placed upon CID officers, ranging from the perceived need in divisional offices to maintain clear up rates at a 'respectable level', to the pressure upon Senior Investigating Officers running major inquiries to make an arrest (both because of the resources tied up in such inquiries and because of media interest in particularly horrific offences). Where the former kinds of pressure are concerned, it seems to us vital to seek new performance measures, based upon quality rather than quantity. Where the latter are concerned, the key requirement is support from higher management: heads of CID should seek to protect SIOs by fielding criticisms from the press and encouraging them to do a thorough and careful job, rather than – as, has too often happened in the past – adding their own voice to the demands that the case be 'cracked'.

iv. Bridging the uniform-CID gap

This is linked to other points already mentioned above – in particular the need for an attack upon the 'elitist culture' of the CID and for interchange of personnel at regular intervals. It also requires closer operational cooperation between CID and uniform officers. At ground level, this can be encouraged by strategies as simple as changing the design of offices: in one subdivision we visited, the CID office was situated away from PCs' normal working areas, the door was always shut, and they found it daunting (or felt unwelcome if they tried) to come in to ask questions about particular cases. By contrast, in another station, the collator's office had been deliberately sited beyond the CID office, so that uniform officers had to walk through the the office in order to use it.

Other practical initiatives to encourage more cooperation in investigative work have included the formation of small mixed squads at divisional level (e.g., street crime squads, vice squads, Drugs Squads) in which PCs work in plain clothes with DCs, or under the supervision of a DS. Further, the requirement now for both police forces and local commanders to set annual 'priorities' and 'objectives' has resulted in CID offices having to contribute to joint initiatives to fulfill them: for example, to take part in coordinated operations against vehicle crime or street robbery and, in one division we know of, to work like uniform officers within a framework of 'geographic policing' (ie with different groups of officers having responsibility, along with their uniform colleagues, for crime in defined sectors of the division).

This shift towards a more planned and coordinated approach to crime control, we were told by divisional commanders, has led to a greater exchange of information and more discussion between themselves and their Detective Inspectors about the day-to-day work of the CID. Daily meetings were now standard practice in most stations we visited, as well as regular joint CID-uniform meetings to discuss policy and review goals and priorities. Even so, the extent to which divisional commanders understood the workings of the CID – or 'wanted to know'- was clearly variable. Like many of the other initiatives and 'good practices' we came across, the effectiveness of such practices is highly dependent upon the commitment of the individual officers involved.

The most radical possibility being floated at the moment in relation to the CID-uniform divide, is the ending of the separate 'CID hierarchy' at force headquarters, bringing local CID offices firmly into the mainstream line management of the force (accountable through divisional commanders to non-specialist managers and policy-makers at headquarters). While there would still be senior detectives available to advise and assist in the investigation of major crime, they would have no management or policy-setting role. This idea was being contemplated very seriously at a high level in one force, and we have a sense that it will gain in momentum over the next few years. The advantages are clear – most obviously, the bridging of the CID-uniform gap and the undermining of the 'elitist' position of the CID, which have caused so much friction over the years – although, the counter-argument, that essential specialist expertise and experience would be lost or seriously diluted, has to be given very careful consideration.

v. Clarifying responsibilities and separating functions

We have identified several areas in which roles have tended to become blurred within the CID, with associated risks to the integrity of investigations. The most obvious, mentioned many times, is the blurring between the operational and supervisory roles of the Detective Sergeant. Our view is that, as far as possible, the DS rank should be supervisory, rather than operational, and that sergeants should not as a rule carry caseloads – a central recommendation of the Metropolitan Police District CIPP report (1989). Further, DSs should be given clear responsibilities – laid down in detailed job descriptions – over a specific group of DCs, and should, within reason, be accountable for their actions.

Within investigations, there are big advantages in the separation of roles, as outlined in our account of the HOLMES system in Chapter Six. Best practice in this regard, in the area of major inquiries, seems to us to include the principle that interviews should be conducted by someone other than the Senior Investigating Officer; the appointment of an independent 'PACE Officer' (rather like an *ad hoc* custody officer, but with a wider brief) to oversee and advise upon procedural correctness; regular and thorough reviews of the state of long-running investigations, preferably by a senior officer from another force, as well as a careful debriefing at the end; and encouragement of advice from the CPS once a clear suspect has emerged.

Obviously, 'ordinary' investigations could not expect anything like this degree of specialisation and commitment of resources, but the principles can still be applied in several ways. For example, one force we visited has adopted a strict policy in child abuse cases for interviews to be conducted by someone other than the officer who has been dealing with the child, accepting that this officer may be emotionally affected as a result. Again, on 'raids' or searches of houses, it is important to appoint an 'exhibits officer', who plays no part in the search but is responsible for all physical evidence found: there is no reason why he or she cannot be a uniform officer.

vi. Seeking new investigative methods

As discussed earlier, many forces are beginning to take seriously the argument that reliance on uncorroborated confessions is a thing of the past and are seeking new strategies for obtaining evidence outside the police station. Surveillance, focussed through improved (and properly researched and graded) criminal intelligence, is widely seen as a way forward, as it offers the chance of catching offenders 'red handed' or in possession of incriminating physical evidence, thus reducing the need for a confession. As we have seen in Chapter Seven, this can be an effective tool, although highly expensive and resource intensive. The chances of 'getting the wrong person' are low, providing some basic checks of information are carried out; and evidence can be gathered systematically in advance of arrest, without the problem that frequently follows a hasty arrest – the race against the 'PACE clock'.

The informant-surveillance model is not, of course, without risks of malpractice. For example, the use of police eye-witness evidence and surveillance logs are areas of potential dispute and fabricated evidence ('gilding the lily'), and where possible need to be backed up with more solid evidence such as photographs. But perhaps the most problematic area is that of handling informants. It seems to us vital, if police forces are going to go down this road, that all CID officers are properly trained in this skill, that clear guidelines are adopted (for example, regarding the circumstances in which informants may be recruited, and the use of 'participating informants') and that tight systems for monitoring contacts and payments are installed. Regional Crime Squad practice provides a good model in this last respect and the set of guidelines recently produced by the ACPO Crime Committee (ACPO 1992) provides a spur to all forces to review and update their procedures. There is also a practical problem in persuading officers to accept the need to *share* information: a widely favoured model is based on the preparation of investigative 'packages' by Intelligence Officers for distribution to CID offices, but this can only be effective if officers feed information to the IOs, rather than keep it to themselves.

vii. Promoting openness

Our final point in this section is one of general principle: that efforts need to be made to promote a spirit of 'openness' in investigations. This might include attaching expert civilians more frequently to investigations as advisers (or even just as observers);more willingness to disclose full evidence to defences (with due regard to sensitive intelligence not directly related to the case); and fostering a 'democratic' rather than 'autocratic' approach among teams working on major inquiries, by which all members are given full opportunities to discuss and to challenge the assumptions of the SIO or policy team. Like many of the other ideas we have put forward, this last one is already being practised in the more forward-looking forces and by the more progressive-minded senior detectives. The challenge is to use the current momentum to institute changes which will outlast the present peak of concern about miscarriages of justice.

Monitoring through 'quality control'

We end this report with a tentative proposal of our own for a radically different system of 'supervision' at ground level. The essence of this proposal, which we emphasise is by no means fully developed, is to move away from reliance upon the 'charismatic' mode of supervision, which depends above all upon faith in the personal qualities of supervisor and supervisee, towards a more impersonal and 'bureaucratic' mode of regulation, based upon the concept of 'quality control'.

Let us begin by briefly repeating the main problems we have identified in the current system. We have described how detectives work with considerable autonomy and have argued that, for the following reasons, current supervisory practices in the CID cannot be viewed as a guarantee of either the thoroughness or the procedural and legal propriety necessary to ensure that investigations do not result in miscarriages of justice:

i. There is considerable pressure to produce 'results' which is passed down the line from headquarters (and, indeed, the Home Office and Inspectorate of Constabulary) to divisional CID management and thence to front line supervisors and DCs. Because of this, rule infraction may be tolerated and justified at ground level in the name of crime control.

ii. The sergeant's role as front line supervisor is undermined by the existence of his or her (often heavy) operational caseload, which not only eats into the time available for supervising subordinate officers, but erodes the distance between ranks (creating loyalties which can conflict with the duty to apply discipline when necessary) and engenders the same emotional commitment to cases and the same pressures to obtain 'results' as are experienced by DCs – and thereby, sometimes, an equal temptation to 'bend the rules'.

iii. The constant drain on supervisory staff to perform other specialist functions means that subordinates are often expected to 'act up' as supervisors. Constables are thus expected to be acting sergeant one day and go back to being constables the next. The same is true at higher ranks, particularly with sergeants 'acting' as inspectors. Under these circumstances, too, the necessary role distancing required to make unpopular decisions is difficult to achieve.

iv. The actual practice of supervision is concerned more with ensuring that officers are working rather than 'skiving', and with checking administrative matters (such as overtime and expenses claims), than with ensuring legal or procedural propriety.

v. The nature of police work, and detective work in particular, makes it very hard actually to supervise the activities of subordinates. Tasks such as statement taking, intelligence gathering and surveillance are low visibility activities, and in these areas the quality and integrity of the investigation depends largely upon the qualities of the individual officer conducting the task, rather than on any supervisory or monitoring role played by a superior officer.

It is in the light of the above points that a key dilemma becomes apparent in trying to implement more effective front line supervision. In order to increase the visibility of the day to day activities of detective constables, one solution is to increase the number of sergeants. However, as the RCS experience discussed in Chapter Seven indicates, a high ratio of sergeants to constables means in practice that sergeants assume a fully investigative and/or 'partner' role, with the attendant danger of the acceptance of informal working practices. An alternative solution is to *decrease* the ratio so that each sergeant has more constables under his or her supervision. This latter route has the benefit of reducing the likelihood of 'incorporation', but carries with it the danger inherent in any line management – that of having to rely upon an upward flow of information from subordinates, with the possible consequence that the supervisor becomes 'out of touch' with the reality on the streets. In spite of this, we are broadly supportive of the recommendations put forward by the Crime Investigation Priority Project (CIPP 1989), and now being implemented in the Metropolitan Police District, that sergeants should assume a greater supervisory role by making them directly responsible for a larger, but specific, group of officers. (It should also be noted that a version of this system was already in operation in one of the forces we looked at, although abstractions and other contingencies made it difficult to follow in practice.)

However, we would suggest that this, in itself, will not be enough. What is needed is a change in managerial culture so that *as much emphasis is placed upon ensuring procedural and legal compliance as upon securing results*. As we have documented, junior and senior management alike maintain that, fundamentally, the guarantee of propriety resides in the leadership and 'tone setting' provided by supervisors, the personal knowledge they have of their subordinates and the trust they consequently feel able to place in their integrity. Trust, however, is a weak guarantee of compliance and, given that trust is largely a private contract, is open to abuse.

To overcome this problem, we suggest that a system of *'quality control'* is required, whereby integrity can be demonstrated, rather than assumed. This system is predicated on two basic principles: *independence* and *randomness*. First, as is to some extent the case in HOLMES inquiries, responsibility for monitoring quality and compliance should be separated from operational investigative procedures; ideally, it should be carried out by dedicated staff, perhaps based in a specialist 'Quality Control Unit'. Second, it should involve the random checking of detective activity. By this we mean that any procedure, such as statement taking or interviewing, undertaken by detectives as part of their day to day work, should have an equal chance of being subject to scrutiny and validation. The choice of officers and which aspects of their work come under scrutiny should not be influenced by fear or favour: *all* officers' work should have the same chance of being selected.

We will give just three examples of areas where such a system would have an impact in helping to secure the quality and integrity of investigations.

i. The monitoring of tape recorded interviews

Although it is claimed that supervisors are now in a position to monitor interviews through listening to the tape, through 'downstream monitoring' or through reading transcripts, we have found little evidence of this occurring. (Indeed, the vast majority of tapes are never heard by *anyone*, as defences request them in very few cases.) This is partly due to lack of time on the part of supervising officers, but a reason more strongly stated was the belief that to monitor interviews in this way would suggest that supervisors did not trust their officers. Further, in the absence of agreed standards as to what constitutes a 'good' or 'bad' interview, judgement about quality, as opposed to procedural impropriety, is, inevitably, personal. However, in some forces, interview training courses have been developed, and these provide models of good practice which could be used to assess the quality of the interview.

Quality control of interviews would, therefore, exhibit the following features. First, tapes and transcripts of interviews would be randomly scrutinised by a Quality Control Unit. This would not only monitor for any breaches of PACE guidelines during interview, but would also determine whether the interview deviated significantly from the model of 'good practice' as determined by training. Second, the officer's own transcript or summary of the tape would be checked against an independent transcript to ensure that it was a true record or accurate precis.

ii. Victim and witness statements

We have argued that victim and witness statements provide a potential weak spot in investigations. A Quality Control Unit might have the job not only of examining samples of statements themselves, but of following up random samples of victims and witnesses, asking them about the manner in which their statements had been taken. The Quality Control Unit would be responsible for ensuring that the contents of these statements were an accurate record of the victim's testimony, that no significant details had been omitted, and no pressure had been brought to bear to 'strengthen' certain aspects of the statement.

iii. HOLMES Systems

In Chapter Six, we described how, in some forces, the headquarters HOLMES unit plays a role in quality control, although at present this is not often formalised. A centralised Quality Control Unit could perform this function in a stronger and more formalised manner. We would suggest two main ways in which it might promote 'good practice'. First, a number of statements could be randomly selected and traced through the system, to ensure that all cross references have been properly indexed and all pertinent actions carried out. Second, at the end of each inquiry, regardless as to whether it had been successful or not, the system should be thoroughly reviewed and a report compiled as to whether procedures have been correctly followed.

We have given only three brief examples of where quality control systems could be introduced to lessen the reliance placed upon trust in ensuring the integrity of investigations. These examples serve only as a starting point. There are, undeniably, other areas where such systems could be put into operation, and our suggestions would also require a great deal of further research and refinement before implementation could be considered. Nevertheless, we believe that their importance lies in the principle of random checks related to *procedural and legal propriety*, and not just to *effectiveness*, as is currently the main purpose of most internal review mechanisms.

We are less sure about the policy which should be followed if and when breaches were discovered. Clearly, it would be invidious to punish officers for every minor error or pecadillo discovered, although disciplinary action would have to follow if more serious failures or misconduct came to light. One possibility, which would go hand in hand with the CIPP model of giving sergeants clear responsibilities vis-a-vis particular groups of DCs, would be to hold supervisors as well as their subordinate officers accountable. Such a system could also include some element of rewarding good practice as well as discouraging the bad. In sum, it would provide a mechanism whereby systematic irregularities could be brought to light, offer a chance that major 'one offs' were discovered, and give supervisors a greater incentive to ensure compliance.

However, such procedures and controls, we repeat, will amount to little unless the fundamental issues of investigative ethics and procedural propriety are addressed in training. At present, formal training is viewed as an adjunct to on-the-job learning and informal socialisation. We believe that detective training should set out a clearly articulated model of good practice and that, before being given the freedom and autonomy necessary to perform detective duties, officers should demonstrate their ability to perform these tasks to an acceptable standard. Thus, after completing formal training, new detectives should be held on probation, for a fixed period, during which time their work should be monitored closely (including through the kind of 'quality control' checks outlined above). This monitoring, perhaps undertaken in conjunction with the training school, would be part of the formal system of assessment, and unacceptable performance would result in failure to be confirmed as a detective.

This last point is linked to the question of selection procedures in general. We support the move in some forces to pass full responsibility for the appointment of CID officers to the force Personnel Department, rather than, as has often been the case, relying principally upon the judgements of Detective Inspectors or Chief Inspectors as to who will make a 'good detective'. Too often, as many officers agreed, such judgements have been made on the sole basis of an officer's ability to produce 'results' and not on how he or she might achieve them.

Concluding Remarks: Crime control and due process

Of course, if something akin to the system we have outlined were adopted, the fundamental problem would remain of the need to control crime and convict the guilty. The most pessimistic adherents of the 'crime control' model described in Chapter Four would argue that the result would be a disastrous reduction in the effectiveness of the CID. Such pessimists include many detectives we spoke to, whose argument was that, if 'the hands of the CID were tied any tighter', morale and motivation would be destroyed and 'the opposition' (the 'villains') would begin to win the 'battle'.

Any successful attempt to solve the problem of dubious practice has to meet this problem head on. First of all, as emphasised previously, it requires a determined search for new methods of investigation, much less reliant on confession evidence alone. This search has already begun in many forces, with the encouragement of 'crime management' methods, based on the improvement and rationalisation of intelligence gathering and on careful analysis of intelligence and crime patterns. This represents a further move away from *ad hoc*, reactive investigation of every individual offence as it is reported, towards longer term planning, the setting of priorities and the mounting of carefully researched operations based on information gathered. It involves more use of methods such as targetted surveillance and a greater focus on physical and documentary evidence. The model is seen in its highest developed form in the 'package' based major operations conducted by Regional Crime Squads, although it is extremely doubtful whether divisional CID offices, with their very different functions and problems, could or should ever aspire to that level of organisation.

Even simplified versions of the above model, we have recognised, are not without their own serious problems. First of all, the proactive investigative methods they rely upon require much more manpower and resources than the reactive system and can cope with far fewer individual crimes and offenders. The alternatives are (a) to increase CID manpower substantially (b) to pass a large proportion of divisional CID officers' present caseloads over to the uniform branch (crucially, the routine visits to the scenes of residential burglaries, which at present take up a great deal of CID time and are often unproductive) or (c) to accept a fall in the numbers of individual crimes cleared up, in return for a smaller number of 'quality' arrests of substantial persistent offenders and a lower proportion of 'dubious' convictions. The first option is probably unrealistic in the present financial climate, but the other two, which are not mutually exclusive, have their attractions. Of course, if PCs are to take on more investigative work, they require training to do so. Such a policy is being followed in some Australian police forces, where all PCs now receive basic detective training.[3] And if the third option is to be adopted, it will require a fundamental change in attitudes to 'effectiveness' and the abandonment of long-accepted ways of measuring it (primarily, the clear-up rate). The huge advantage of the latter change would be a reduction in the 'pressure for results' which still dominates the detective working environment.

Secondly, the kinds of methods on which these new approaches to investigation would be based, while less likely to result in wrongful convictions (provided that the intelligence on which operations is based is properly checked) raise their own questions about *civil liberties*. At their most sophisticated level, proactive techniques include the use of telephone tapping, access to bank accounts, 'deep cover' work by police officers, the use of 'participating informants', 'sting operations' and other highly controversial methods of obtaining information. They also include the danger of slipping into the kind of *agent provocateur* methods which caused so much concern at the very birth of the CID. In the USA, and in many European countries, such issues are already arousing considerable concern, particularly in relation to major anti-drugs operations[4]. They will, we suggest, attract growing interest over the next few years in relation to major police operations in Britain and, cross-border, into Europe (cf. Levi and Maguire 1992). Although the more sophisticated of these methods are unlikely to be used at divisional level, one can easily envisage

---

[3] See Bradley (1991).
[4] This formed a major theme at the Law and Society Conference in Amsterdam in 1991, where Gary Marx and Cyrille Feinhaut, two leading writers in this field, commissioned a number of well-informed papers (see also Block 1992).

controversy over 'sting' operations and perceived provocations to commit crime, as has occurred in the USA at local level.

Most important, though, the kinds of investigative methods being advocated will raise major questions about relations and contacts between officers and informants, where the need for control is a clear one. Here, as we have already argued, a great deal can be learned from the experiences of the Regional Crime Squads in regulating such contacts (by the use of registration, contact forms, supervision of payments, and so on).

In conclusion, although this study has to a large extent had a negative focus, we believe that there is at present a strong current of desire for change running through the police service, fuelled by the despair that many honest officers have felt at the revelations of incompetence and malpractice which have assailed the police in recent years and months. If this desire can be harnessed in a positive fashion, and internal initiatives already in motion can be built upon, there is some cause for optimism that the problems we have outlined, although profound and extremely resistant to solution, may be tackled in a meaningful way.

BIBLIOGRAPHY

ACPO (1990) *Strategic Policy Document* London: Metropolitan Police District.

ACPO (1992) *National Guidelines on the Use and Management of Informants* ACPO Crime Committee Working Party on the Management of Informants (unpublished).

Allason, R. (1983) *The Branch: A History of the Metropolitan Police Special Branch* London: Secker & Warburg.

Ascoli, D. (1979) *The Queen's Peace* London: Hamilton.

Audit Commission (1990) *Effective Policing – Performance Review in Police Forces* Police Papers Number 8 Dec. 1990. London: Audit Commission.

Bennett, T. (1990) *Measuring the Quality of Police Service and Customer Satisfaction.* (Report to Home Office – unpublished).

Block, A. (1992) *Special Issue: Issues and Theories on Covert Policing* Crime, Law and Social Change, Vol 18. Nos 1–2, September 1992.

Bottomley, A. K. and **Coleman, T.** (1981) *Understanding Crime Rates* Aldershot: Gower.

Bottomley, A. K., Coleman, C., Dixon, D., Gill, M. and **Wall, D.** (1991) *The Impact of PACE* University of Hull: Centre for Criminology and Criminal Justice.

Bottomley, A. K., Coleman, C., Dixon, D., Gill, M. and **Wall, D.** (1991a) 'The detention of suspects in police custody' *British Journal of Criminology* vol 31 no 4, 347–64.

Bradley, D. (1991) *Investigators Course* New South Wales: New South Wales Police Academy.

Brodeur, J. (1981) 'Legitimizing police deviance' in C. Shearing (ed) *Organizational Police Deviance* Toronto: Butterworth.

Brown, D. (1989) *Detention at the police station under PACE* Home Office Research Study No. 104. London: HMSO.

Brown, D. (1991) *Investigating Burglary: The Effects of PACE* Home Office Research Study No. 123. London: HMSO.

Burge, D. (1989) *Activity Indicators for Police Forces* Paper presented at the Statistics Users Society. (Manuscript, Unpublished).

Burrows, J. (1986) *Burglary: Police Actions and Victims' Views* Home Office Research Paper 37. London: Home Office.

Burrows, J. and **Tarling, R.** (1987) "The investigation of crime in England and Wales" *British Journal of Criminology*, Vol 27, No. 3.

Chatterton, M. (1987) 'Front line supervision in the British police service' in G. Gaskell and R. Benewick (eds) *The Crowd in Contemporary Britain* London: Sage.

CIPP (1989) *Report of the Crime Investigation Priority Project Team* London: Metropolitan Police (unpublished).

Colman, T. (1989) *Incident into Evidence: Operational Police Skills* Maidenhead: McGraw-Hill.

Cox, B., Shirley, J. and **Short, M.** (1977) *The Fall of Scotland Yard* Harmondsworth: Penguin.

Critchley, T. (1967) *A History of Police in England and Wales* London: Constable.

Crust, P. (1975) *Criminal Investigation Project* Home Office Police Services Unit (Unpublished).

Gibb-Gray, B. (1990) 'Reorganising crime investigation' *Policing* Vol 6, Spring 1990, pp.355–62.

Gouldner, A. (1954) *Patterns of Industrial Bureaucracy* New York: Free Press.

Greenwood, P., Chaiken, J. and **Petersilia, J.** (1977) *The Criminal Investigation Process* Lexington, Mass: DC Heath.

Harper, R. (1991) 'The computer game: detectives, suspects and technology' *British Journal of Criminology* Vol 31, 3 292–307.

Hobbs, R. (1988) *Doing the Business* Oxford: Clarendon Press.

Hobbs, R. and **Maguire, M.** (1989) "Detective work: a review of the literature" in *Report of the Priority Project on the Investigation of Crime* London: Metropolitan Police.

Holdaway, S. (1983) *Inside the British Police* Oxford: Blackwell.

Home Office (1990) *Criminal Statistics, England and Wales, 1989* London: HMSO.

Home Office (1991) *Police and Criminal Evidence Act 1984 (s.66): Codes of Practice* London: HMSO.

Hough, M. (1987) "Thinking about effectiveness" *British Journal of Criminology*, Vol 27, No. 1. pp.70–79.

Irving, B. and **Hilgendorf, L.** (1980) *Police Interrogation* Royal Commission on Criminal Procedure, Research Study No. 1.

Irving, B. and **McKenzie, I.** (1989) *Police Interrogation: the Effects of PACE 1984* London: Police Foundation.

Irving, B. and **Dunnighan, C.** (1992) *Human Factors in the Quality Control of CID Investigators* Report to Royal Commission on Criminal Justice. forthcoming London: HMSO.

Jacobs, J. (1969) 'Symbolic bureaucracy' *Social Forces* 47, 413–22.

Kaye, T. (1991) *Unsafe and Unsatisfactory? Report of the Independent Inquiry into the Working Practices of the West Midlands Serious Crime Squad* London: Civil Liberties Trust.

Kinsey, R., Lea, J. and **Young, J.** (1986) *Losing the Fight Against Crime*, Oxford: Blackwell.

Leng, R. (1992) 'The Right to Silence in Police Interrogation' Report to Royal Commission on Criminal Justice. forthcoming London: HMSO.

Levi, M. and **Maguire, M.** (1992) 'Cross-border crime and policing in Europe' in J. Bailey (ed.) *Social Europe* London: Longman Press.

Love, S. (1990) *A Guide to Designing Performance Indicators.* Cambridge: HMIC.

LSPU (1984) *Police Complaints: A Fresh Approach* Police Monitoring and Research Group. London: London Strategic Policy Unit.

Lustgarten, L. (1986) *The Governance of Police* London: Sweet and Maxwell.

Maguire, M. (1982) *Burglary in a Dwelling: The Offence, the Offender and the Victim.* London: Heinemann

Maguire, M. (1985) 'The impact of burglary: questions for the police and criminal justice system' in *Coping with Burglary* (ed R. Clarke and T. Hope) Lancaster: Kluwer Nijhoff.

Maguire, M. (1988) "Effects of the PACE provisions on detention and questioning: some preliminary findings" *British Journal of Criminology* vol 28, pp 19–43.

Maguire, M. and **Corbett, C.** (1991) *A Study of the Police Complaints System* London: HMSO.

Maguire, M. (1991) 'The needs and rights of victims of crime' *Crime and Justice* Vol 14. Chicago: University of Chicago Press.

Maguire, M., Noaks, L., Hobbs, R. and **Brearley, N.** (1992) *Assessing Detective Effectiveness* Cardiff: Social Research Unit, SOCAS, University of Wales.

Manning, P. (1977) *Police Work* Cambridge, Mass: MIT Press.

Mark, R. (1978) *In the Office of Constable* London: Collins.

Marx, G. (1989) *Undercover: Police Surveillance in America.* Berkeley, Calif: University of California.

Mawby, R. (1979) *Policing the City.* London: Saxon House.

McBarnet, D. (1981) *Conviction, Law, the State and the Construction of Justice* London: Macmillan.

McCabe, S. and **Sutcliffe, F.** (1976) *Defining Crime* Oxford: Centre for Criminological Research.

McConville, M., Sanders, A. and **Leng, R.** (1991) *The Case for the Prosecution* London: Routledge.

Morgan, B. (1990) *The Police Function and the Investigation of Crime* Aldershot: Avebury.

Moston, S., Stephenson, G. and **Williamson, T.** (1990) *Police Interrogation Styles and Suspect Behaviour* University of Kent: Institute of Social and Applied Psychology.

Moston, S. and **Stephenson, G.** and **Williamson, T.** (1992) 'The effects of case characteristics on suspect behaviour during Police questioning'. *British Journal Criminology Vol 32 No. 1 Winter 1992.*

Moston, S. and **Stephenson, G.** (1992) *'Interviews with Suspects Outside the Police Station'.* Report to Royal Commission on Criminal Justice. forthcoming London: HMSO.

MPD (1991) *Plus Briefing: A Summary of Component Activities* London: Metropolitan Police District.

Norris, C. (1989) 'Avoiding trouble: the patrol officer's perception of the public' in M. Weatheritt (ed) *Police Research: Some Future Prospects* Aldershot: Avebury.

Prothero, M. (1931) *The History of the Criminal Investigation Department at Scotland Yard* London: Herbert Jenkins.

Punch, M. (ed. 1983) *Control in the Police Organization* Cambridge, Mass: MIT Press.

Reiner, R. (1988) "Keeping The Home Office happy: can police effectiveness be measured by performance indicators?" *Policing* Vol.4 No.1 Spring 1988

Shapland, J., Willmore, J. and **Duff, P.** (1985) *Victims in the Criminal Justice System* Aldershot: Gower.

Shapland, J. and **Vagg, J.** (1988) *Policing by the Public* London: Routledge.

Short, M. (1991) *Lundy: The Destruction of Scotland Yard's Finest Detective* London: Grafton Books.

Sinclair, I. and **Miller, C.** (1984) *Measures of Police Effectiveness and Efficiency.* Home Office Research and Planning Unit Paper 25 London: Home Office.

Skolnick, J. (1966) *Justice Without Trial: Law Enforcement in a Democratic Society* New York: Wiley.

Smith, D. and **Gray, J.** (1985) *Police and People in London: The PSI Report* Aldershot: Gower.

Steer, D. (1980) *Uncovering Crime: The Police Role* Royal Commission on Criminal Procedure, Research Study No. 7. London: HMSO.

Tarling, R. and **Burrows, J.** (1985) 'The work of detectives' in Heal, K., Tarling, R. and Burrows, J. *Policing Today* London: HMSO.

Thornton, G. (1989) *The Role of the Criminal Investigation Department: Present Performance and Future Prospects* Unpublished M.A. Thesis, Faculty of Social and Economic Studies, University of Manchester.

Wensley, F. (1931) *Detective Days* London: Cassell.

Young, M. (1991) *An Inside Job* Oxford: Clarendon Press.

Wright, A. and **Waymont, A.** (1992) *Management of Drugs Squads and Drugs Wings: Interim Report* London: Police Foundation (unpublished).